After S...
The Pres...
of British ...theism

After Secularisation:
The Present and Future
of British Catholicism

Stephen Bullivant
Hannah Vaughan-Spruce
Bernadette Durcan

Cover image: *The Stations of the Cross through Soho, London*.
Photo by Isaac Withers © 2024 St Patrick's Church, Soho Square.

After Secularisation was first published in 2025 by CTS Press.
CTS Press is an imprint of The Catholic Truth Society.
42-46 Harleyford Road London SE11 5AY
Tel: 020 7640 0042. *www.ctsbooks.org*
© 2025 The Incorporated Catholic Truth Society.
All rights reserved.

ISBN 978-1-78469-853-9

Contents

About the Authors vii

Acknowledgements.. ix

Introduction 1

1. Parishes 20

2. Youth Movements and Initiatives 53

3. Diasporas 85

4. University Chaplaincies and CathSocs 111

5. Latin Massers (and the Liturgical Long Tail) 137

6. Epilogue: A British Spring?..165

Appendix: Historical Mass Attendance Statistics 170

About the Authors

Stephen Bullivant is Professor of Theology and the Sociology of Religion at St Mary's University, Twickenham, and Professorial Research Fellow in Theology and Sociology at the University of Notre Dame Australia, Sydney. He directs the Benedict XVI Centre for Religion and Society at both institutions. Recent books include: *Catholics in Contemporary Britain: Faith, Society, Politics* (Oxford University Press, 2022; co-authored with Ben Clements); and *Vatican II: A Very Short Introduction* (Oxford University Press, 2023; co-authored with Shaun Blanchard).

Hannah Vaughan-Spruce is Executive Director of Global Mission at Divine Renovation, a ministry that exists to help parishes move from maintenance to mission. She read Theology at Cambridge and was awarded her PhD from St Mary's University, Twickenham, in the area of sociology of religion and theology. She has published a number of books, including *Why Catholics Leave, What They Miss, and How They Might Return* (Paulist Press, 2019; co-authored with Stephen Bullivant, Catherine Knowles, and Bernadette Durcan), and *Handbook for Catechists* (CTS, 2018). She is a consecrated virgin of the Archdiocese of Southwark.

Bernadette Durcan is a PhD candidate with the Benedict XVI Centre at St Mary's University, Twickenham. She holds an MA in Social Research Methods from the University of Liverpool. Her previous book is *Why Catholics Leave, What They Miss, and Why They Might Return* (Paulist Press, 2019; co-authored with Stephen Bullivant, Catherine Knowles, and Hannah Vaughan-Spruce).

Acknowledgements

This work was made possible thanks to the generosity of Porticus UK in supporting the 'Seeds of Hope: Catholic Growth in the UK' (2019–2023) project. We are hugely grateful to them for their support and patience, especially in navigating the Covid-19 pandemic and its various impacts. At Porticus, special gratitude is owed to Jane Leek and Will Mattiello-Kent.

As is evident in the following pages, we have relied throughout on the help, big and small, of a vast number of people: interviewees, 'gatekeepers' of various kinds, priests, religious, lay chaplains, parish and diocesan staff, other scholars, strangers (some of whom we now call friends) emailed for this or that stat, and members of the various congregations and groups up and down the country who have been unfailingly welcoming and forbearing of the 'spies' (cf. chapter four) in their midst. We thank several people individually in the footnotes, for 'some definite service' or other. We also owe particular thanks to Emily Nelson, who has been instrumental at various points of this project.

On a more personal level:

Stephen wishes to thank his wife, Joanna, for everything. Grace, Alice, Francis, and Leo, in various combinations, were more or less willing/bribable confederates on all manner of 'daddy adventures' (a phrase they now treat with a good deal of suspicion). Thanks to them too.

Hannah wishes to thank the inspirational leaders of parishes and young people who are true heroes behind the shoots of new life we are seeing. Their courage and determination to innovate comes often at personal cost and yet, without their experimentations, learnings and even failures, we in the Church would not have the pathfinders ahead of us, showing us how to adapt and discover new paths in a challenging environment. They deserve our heartfelt honour and thanks.

Berna would like to thank her parents, Michael and Lynda; Rosie and Riz for their limitless hospitality whilst conducting fieldwork; Fran and Robin; Dr Ciara Durcan for her companionship on the academic voyage; Dom; and Jamie, who is serendipity in human form. Your collective love and patience are much appreciated.

Introduction

'I've seen the future of British Catholicism', I[1] messaged a couple of friends via Facebook. 'It looks like a rainy day in West Bromwich.'

This particular rainy day was a Saturday in June 2019. More importantly, it was a 'Second Saturday', which is how AFCM bills the monthly conventions it's held since 2010 (pandemics permitting).[2] These 'family friendly gatherings include lively praise and worship, Holy Mass, Healing Services, Inspiring Bible Talks, and Eucharistic Adoration',[3] and typically run from 8am to 4pm. Confessions are offered throughout the day, in a range of languages. Fasting is strongly encouraged: those needing to eat are welcome to bring their own food, but it is not served or sold otherwise. None of this, one might think, is exactly designed to pull in the crowds. And yet, each month roughly 2-3000 people of all ages descend on this West Midlands conference centre, conveniently situated just off the M5. Parking is free, but only if you get there early enough; fourteen coaches, from all over the country, accounted for a fair chunk of the space available. Not wanting to trek too far in the drizzle, I joined other attendees' cars – readily identifiable by the Marian bumper stickers, rosaries dangling from rearview mirrors, and the dashboard saint statuettes – cramming the surrounding side

---

1   In this particular case, SB. Please see 'Note' at the end of this Introduction.
2   The organization was previously known as Sehion Ministries, as indeed it was in 2019.
3   AFCM UK, 'Second Saturday Conventions', 2024, <*https://www.afcmuk.org/event/second-saturday-convention/*>.

streets. Fortunately, the distinctive yellow parking fine notice that greeted me on my return was well and truly worth it.

Heading inside, the conference foyer is busy with activity: milling families, people browsing bookstalls, groups of teenagers chatting among themselves, all evidently 'at home' here. In a quiet(er) corner there's a makeshift confessional – i.e., a couple of chairs – where a girl, who looks to be about 17, is tearfully pouring her heart out to a young priest. Fifteen other teenagers, standing in line a short distance away, all tactfully pretend not to notice. Elsewhere, an even longer line of both individuals and couples wait at an impromptu 'healing/prayer station', of the sort one sometimes sees set up by Pentecostal churches in town centres, to talk and/or pray with one of a team of lay 'ministers'. The conference itself, a rolling programme of talks, music, and religious services (Mass, Adoration, led Rosary), is split into two tracks: Malayalam (the main language spoken in Kerala, southern India) in the main auditorium, and English in a large marquee erected outside. When I look in on the former in the mid-afternoon, I count well over a thousand people, almost all of whom are unsurprisingly of Indian origin, listening intently to an energetic Bible study by a priest involving much audience participation, and with regular musical interludes performed by a house band. For one well-used to casting a 'sociological eye'[4] over Catholic gatherings in Britain, two things in particular stand out: the wide mix of ages with no group obviously under- or over-represented, and the presence of large numbers of men. Meanwhile in the English revival-style tent, a young Irish priest is delivering a homely piece of catechesis, replete with jokes, personal anecdotes, and the occasional phrase of Malayalam. Almost full, it contains a much broader ethnic mix than the main hall. Plenty of (mostly younger) British Indians are here too, but so are

---

[4] Cf. Randall Collins, 'The Sociological Eye and Its Blinders', *Contemporary Sociology*, 27.1 (1998), 2–7.

plenty of whites, blacks, and South-East Asians. Among the whites, a fair proportion have Irish accents, with many likely to be from the Traveller community, who remain one of the more steadfastly devout segments of the Irish diaspora.[5] One middle-aged woman I spoke to had come down from Barnsley that day, a 200 mile roundtrip: 'we never miss it'.

AFCM UK is part of Anointing Fire Catholic Ministries, a movement within the Syro-Malabar Catholic Church. This is one of the twenty-three Eastern Catholic Churches who, along with the western Latin Church, make up the Catholic Church. The Syro-Malabars are, along with the Syro-Malankara Catholic Church, one of two Eastern Churches rooted in Kerala, India, but present in Malayalee diaspora communities throughout the world. We will have much more to say about both Churches, plus several other Eastern Catholic Churches active – in some cases, very active – in Britain, in chapter three.

Needless to say, this rainy day in West Bromwich hardly depicts the *full* present or future of Britain's Catholic community. How could it? Roughly 3.6 million British adults identify as Catholic on surveys (though perhaps double that number were baptised Catholic, and hence *are* Catholics, whether they like it or not, on the Church's own sacramental definition of belonging).[6] Of these, a little over half a million can be found at Mass on any given Sunday. First, second, and/or third-generation British Indians, Irish Travellers, and assorted others for whom AFCM's signature blend of charismatic, devotional Catholicism is 'their thing' make up only a small proportion of the whole. But, in a sense, that's rather our

---

[5] E.g., 'Many Irish Travellers retain a strong Catholic faith – I don't think I've ever met as many devout people as I have in getting to know Gypsy and Traveller families over the past few years'; Katharine Quarmby, *No Place to Call Home: Inside the Real Lives of Gypsies and Travellers* (London: Oneworld, 2013), Introduction.

[6] Ben Clements and Stephen Bullivant, *Catholics in Contemporary Britain: Faith, Society, Politics* (Oxford: Oxford University Press, 2022), 9-16.

point. Contemporary British Catholicism comprises a significant number of distinct, diverse strands. For a variety of reasons, several of these are showing a good deal of resilience, and even growth, in the midst of a heavily secularised wider culture. Our main aim in writing this book is to make some of these stories better known. These case studies are, we think, interesting and important in their own right: the Catholic Church, despite being 'Britain's largest Christian denomination in terms of actual attendance at weekly services',[7] is notably under-represented in studies of British religion. But we also hope that at least some of what these British Catholics are getting right might be applicable much more widely, both at home and abroad.

This is, moreover, an opportune moment for such a book. It is no secret that Christianity in Britain is, according to traditional indicators of pastoral health such as baptisms, confirmations, weddings, and church attendance, several decades into a period of slow, steady shrinkage.[8] In the blunt assessment of one recent study, 'Christianity was once powerful, persuasive, and popular and now it is none of those things.'[9] While Catholicism is by no means the worst affected of Britain's Christian denominations, it too has seen significant declines. Here, let us mention just the most salient indicator: 'typical Sunday' Mass attendance. Just prior to the pandemic, in 2019, this stood at roughly 829,000 across England, Wales, and Scotland. In itself, this is not a small number of Mass-goers.

---

[7] Ben Clements and Stephen Bullivant, 'Why Younger Catholics Seem More Committed: Survivorship Bias and/or "Creative Minority" Effects among British Catholics', *Journal for the Scientific Study of Religion*, 61.2 (2022), 450–75.

[8] In impressive detail, see Clive D. Field, *Counting Religion in Britain, 1970-2020: Secularization in Statistical Context* (Oxford: Oxford University Press, 2021). For a helpful summary of Catholic trends, see Timothy Kinnear, 'Statistical Appendices', in Alana Harris (ed.), *The Oxford History of British and Irish Catholicism, Vol. 5: Recapturing the Apostolate of the Laity, 1914-2021* (Oxford: Oxford University Press, 2023), 357–76.

[9] Steve Bruce, *British Gods: Religion in Modern Britain* (Oxford: Oxford University Press, 2020), 252.

But it is a good deal fewer than the 1,265,000 who were there in 1999, or the 1,940,000 nineteen years before that, in 1980. Post-pandemic, in 2022, Mass attendance in Britain was officially counted at 592,000.[10]

In some of our previous works, we have explored various facets of all this in much detail.[11] If the present volume strikes a rather more hopeful tone, therefore, we can hardly be accused of ignorance or naivety. Secularisation is the single biggest fact of recent British religious history. The country is significantly less religious – and not merely 'differently' religious – than it was not all that long ago. Recent British Catholic history is no exception.

And yet: it remains the case that, alongside (or perhaps hidden within) these overall trends, there is a great deal else going on. Decline has not happened uniformly, and some sectors of the Church are not just surviving but thriving. What's more, even as overall decline continues for some years more, these sectors of resistance are, slowly but surely, laying the groundwork for a future upturn. Contrary to some suggestions, present trends will not continue for ever. They rarely do, at least not for ever. The Church is not headed towards some 'extinction' point at any time, let alone (as on one estimate) by the early 2060s.[12] Decline will bottom out at some point and probably, at least to some degree, reverse.

---

[10] Mass count figures in this paragraph have been given to the nearest 1,000. More precise (though not necessarily more accurate) figures are given as an Appendix, based on a variety of official sources.

[11] See Stephen Bullivant, Catherine Knowles, Hannah Vaughan-Spruce, and Bernadette Durcan, *Why Catholics Leave, What They Miss, and How They Might Return* (Mahwah, NJ: Paulist Press, 2019), and Stephen Bullivant, *Mass Exodus: Catholic Disaffiliation in Britain and America since Vatican II* (Oxford: Oxford University Press, 2019).

[12] John Hayward, 'Growth, Decline and Extinction of UK Churches', available online at: <https://churchmodel.org.uk/2022/05/15/growth-decline-and-extinction-of-uk-churches/>. It is worth saying that Dr Hayward's overall work on church growth modelling has a great deal to recommend it, and churches can learn much from this kind of approach. However, the specific prediction made here about the Catholic Church is way off for several reasons, most obviously because the model used fails to take into account immigration.

When in the course of the next few decades that occurs, and *how well-equipped* the Church is to bounce back, will largely depend on how well the Church *now* recognises, resources, learns from, and leans into some of the groups and communities we will meet in the coming pages – and others like them.

That, at least, is the guiding argument of this book. The research for it began, formally, in 2019 (though we are, of course, also drawing on much of our own prior research and experiences), thanks to the generous funding and support of Porticus UK. The project has taken us the length and breadth of Britain, including to a great many out-of-the-way places where the uninitiated might not think to look for the seeds of a coming Catholic renewal. The Covid-19 pandemic both disrupted our fieldwork plans, and changed the field itself.[13] It also made this kind of research all the more urgent and, we trust, useful. Accordingly, we extended our research longer than originally planned, right up until the time of writing in late 2023 and early 2024. The full, long-term effects of the pandemic on British religion will not become fully clear for some decades.[14] Nevertheless, the pastoral situation has now mostly settled down into a post-pandemic 'new normal', and it is this situation that we are addressing.

Creative Minority Effects

Although interrelated, the chapters in this book function as a series of separate case studies: 'deep dives' into one subgroup, or set of related subgroups, of British Catholicism at a time. Uniting them,

---

[13] E.g., Bernadette Durcan, 'Negotiating the Field through Necessity: Transformations in Approach to Ethnographic Research on Religious Studenthood during COVID-19', *Sentio* 3 (2021), 101–4.

[14] For example, there is a wealth of social-scientific evidence on the importance of childhood religious practice, not least churchgoing, in predicting adult religiosity (see footnote 24, below). Even for the young families who have since returned to church (which is by no means all of those who were there before), it remains to be seen what subtle, long-term impacts the sustained period of on-again, off-again church closures and/or significant restrictions (booking in advance, locking out latecomers etc.) might have.

however, is a specific sociological thesis, parts of which we have worked out more fully in other publications.[15] This thesis is mostly implicit in the chapters themselves, but here we'd like to take the opportunity to set it out explicitly.

Let us begin with an interesting fact. According to a nationally representative survey of British Catholics in late 2019, younger Catholics (i.e., those aged 18-44) are *more* committed than are older Catholics (i.e., 45+) on key indicators including Mass attendance, frequency of going to Confession, and doctrinal orthodoxy. For example, 41% of 18-24 year-olds and 45% of 25-34 year-olds reported attending Mass on a weekly basis, compared to just 17% of 55-64 year-olds and 25% of over-65s. Likewise, 63% of 18-24s and 59% of 35-44s said they 'definitely' or 'probably' believe in the 'Real Presence of Christ's body and blood in the Eucharist', compared to 41% of 55-64s and 46% of over-65s.[16] True, there is a good deal of room for improvement in all those figures, but the clear positive correlation between youthfulness and committedness is plain (and holds when controlling for other factors).

These findings, however counterintuitive and indeed contrary to the findings of earlier studies,[17] in fact make perfect sense. They are the product of a couple of basic facts.

The first is that younger Catholics have, thanks to relentless secularisation, been raised in a much less religious world than were older Catholics. On average, they are less likely to have grown

---

[15] Most importantly, in Hannah Vaughan-Spruce, '"Relationships Are the Currency of Mission": The Impact of Parish Priest Transitions on Evangelization', *Catholic Social Science Review* 27 (2022), 69–79; Hannah Vaughan-Spruce, 'From Sacred Canopy to Sacred Umbrellas: Cultural Characteristics of Parishes that Thrive', PhD thesis, St Mary's University, 2021; Clements and Bullivant, 'Why Younger Catholics Seem More Committed'; Clements and Bullivant, *Catholics in Contemporary Britain*; and Stephen Bullivant, 'Mass Markets and the "Liturgical Long Tail"', *Antiphon* 26/1 (2022), 1–25.

[16] Data taken from Clements and Bullivant, *Catholics in Contemporary Britain*, 42–5, 77.

[17] E.g., Michael P. Hornsby-Smith, *Roman Catholics in England: Studies in Social Structure since the Second World War* (Cambridge: Cambridge University Press, 1987), 45.

up in a thick Catholic subculture than were, say, their parents or (especially) their grandparents. And if seeing oneself as having no religion is the default 'cultural norm'[18] for Britons as a whole these days, then it is all the more so for those in their late-teens, twenties, and thirties. Surveys have shown that around two-thirds of British 18-34 year-olds identify as having no religion, for example.[19]

What this means is that, in order to still be 'ticking the Catholic box' (i.e., to end up being counted in surveys *of* Catholics), younger adults are necessarily more likely to *mean something* by it. If they didn't, then they, like a large proportion of their fellow cradle-Catholic peers (including from their own families and Catholic schools), would have simply stopped ticking the box long ago. That is to say, younger Catholics are much less likely to identify as such for purely 'cultural' or 'tribal' reasons, than are older Catholics.[20]

This has a dual effect on our data. The first, probably biggest, and pastorally least encouraging effect is that it serves to 'inflate' the averages for younger Catholics, due to the least committed cradle Catholics (i.e., those so uncommitted that they no longer think of themselves as being Catholic at all) being self-excluded from the sample. Meanwhile those who remain to be counted are the relative hard core. This is a case of what statisticians call survivorship bias, and it's important that we are aware of it.[21]

---

[18] Linda Woodhead, 'The rise of "no religion" in Britain: The emergence of a new cultural majority', *Journal of the British Academy* 4 (2016), 245–61

[19] David Voas and Steve Bruce, 'Religion', in J. Curtice, E. Clery, J. Perry, M. Phillips, and N. Rahim (eds) *British Social Attitudes: The 36th Report* (London: National Centre for Social Research), 17–38, at 15; Stephen Bullivant, *Europe's Young Adults and Religion: Findings from the European Social Survey (2014–16) to inform the 2018 Synod of Bishops* (Benedict XVI Centre for Religion and Society; Institut Catholique de Paris, 2018), 9.

[20] See Michael P. Hornsby-Smith, 'The Changing Identity of Catholics in England', in Simone Coleman and Peter Collins (ed.), *Religion, Identity and Change: Perspectives on Global Transformations* (Abingdon: Routledge), pp. 42–56.

[21] For a non-technical explanation of survivorship bias, and its relevance to several fields, see Jordan Ellenberg, *How Not to Be Wrong: The Hidden Maths of Everyday Life* (London: Allen Lane, 2014), 3–10.

The second effect, however, is critical for understanding what's going on in many of the case-studies to follow. Precisely because being religious is so 'alien'[22] to wider British culture, especially among younger adults, then it means that those who *are* must personally own it. Or to put it another way, those who are still here at the end of sixty-odd years of decline, are here for a reason. 'A dead thing can go with the stream, but only a living thing can go against it', as GK Chesterton once famously remarked.[23] What this means in practice is that if you are in your late-teens, twenties, or thirties, and are still going to Mass, then you are swimming strongly against the cultural stream, and likely have been for some years. There could be multiple reasons for this. Perhaps your family has somehow kept up a much higher-than-average level of religious belief and practice than others (although this in itself is no guarantee).[24] Perhaps you are a first- or second-generation immigrant from one of the very many more-religious-than-Britain countries, and hence were raised in a much richer Catholic subculture than most 'native' cradle Catholics are (see below, and also chapter three). Or perhaps you are a convert from a different denomination or religion (or no religion), or else a 'revert' raised in a weakly Catholic household,

---

[22] Steve Bruce, 'Late Secularization and Religion as Alien', *Open Theology* 1 (2014), 13–23.

[23] GK Chesterton, *The Everlasting Man* (London: Hodder and Stoughton, 1927), 297.

[24] There is a wealth of studies showing the important of family religious practice in childhood as a predictor of adult religiosity. Two especially important and helpful ones are: Vern L. Bengtson, Norella M. Putney, and Susan Harris, *Families and Faith: How Religion is Passed Down Across Generations* (New York: Oxford University Press, 2013); and David Voas and Ingrid Storm, 'National Context, Parental Socialization, and the Varying Relationship between Religious Belief and Practice', *Journal for the Scientific Study of Religion* 60/1 (2021), 189–97.

Even with regular family religious practice growing up, however, some studies have estimated only a coin-flip chance of becoming a religious practising adult oneself. E.g., 'If neither parent attends at least once a month, the chances of the child doing so are negligible: less than 3 percent. If both parents attend at least monthly, there is a 46 percent chance that the child will do so. Where just one parent attends, the likelihood is halved to 23 percent' (David Voas and Alisdair Crockett, 'Religion in Britain: Neither Believing nor Belonging', *Sociology* 39/1, 11-28, at 21).

with some particular tale of Providence to tell.[25] We know committed young Catholics from all of these categories.

Here's where things get interesting. What happens when a group of these deviantly religious, committed young Catholic swimmers-against-the-stream get together? This happens quite naturally at, say, university chaplaincies or CathSocs (see chapter four), certain movements or conferences (see chapter two), or else at particular kinds of parishes or liturgies (see chapters one and five). It also, of course, happens a good deal online, on Facebook, WhatsApp, Twitter/X, and other platforms. Beliefs or identities are most easily held when they are shared with others. It is much easier to be distinctive, and proudly so, when one belongs to a mutually validating and reinforcing 'tribe' of like-minded others.[26] Everyone encourages everyone else, creating a robust subculture of people well aware of how culturally weird they are, but all the more rooted in being so. (A nice illustration of this comes from the 2019 survey cited above: frequency of Mass attendance is strongly correlated with the

---

[25] Susan Longhurst, 'Who Joins the Catholic Church and Why?': Exploring the Nature of Catholic Conversion for Individuals in the Archdiocese of Southwark', PhD thesis, St Mary's University, 2022.

[26] This is a basic truth of social life, reflecting very normal aspects of social psychology: 'Humans are not exactly lemmings, but they are easily influenced by the statements and deeds of others' (Richard Thaler and Cass R. Sunstein, *Nudge: Improving Decisions About Health, Wealth, and Happiness* [New Haven, CT: Yale University Press, 2008], chap. 3). It applies to all sorts of things, from playground peer pressure, to being a superfan of Bob Dylan or Taylor Swift, to eco-activism (as a general rule, you don't glue your face to the road during rush-hour without a close-knit peer group of others who think it's a good idea), to devoting one's evenings to writing Harry Potter fanfic. There is, naturally, a large literature on subcultural identity theory.

More generally, there is a large literature on the influence of 'social networks' or 'plausibility structures' on all manner of aspects of belief, belonging, and behaviour, religious or otherwise. Our thinking on these topics has been particularly influenced in various ways by: Peter Berger and Thomas Luckmann, *The Social Construction of Reality: A Treatise in the Sociology of Knowledge* (New York: Anchor Books, 1966); Peter Berger, *The Sacred Canopy: Elements of a Sociological Theory of Religion* (New York: Doubleday, 1967); and Nicholas A. Christakis and James H. Fowler, *Connected: The Surprising Power of Our Social Networks and How They Shape Our Lives* (New York: Little, Brown, and Co., 2009).

number of close Catholic friends a person has.[27]) They are, as per Christian Smith's famous description of American Evangelicals a quarter-century ago, 'embattled but thriving'.[28] These are ideas to which we will return at several points throughout the book.

While these kinds of social and cultural dynamics are surely not unique to Catholicism (somewhat similar dynamics can be seen at work among young British Evangelicals and Muslims, for example[29]), there are good reasons for thinking that they might be particularly applicable to Catholic contexts, especially in the West. The phenomenon of 'highly religious young Catholics'[30] has recently drawn academic and media attention in a number of countries, including the USA, Italy, and Australia.[31] It therefore makes sense for us to label this as a 'creative minority effect', adopting a phrase with currency within Catholic circles thanks to the late Pope Benedict's employment of it.

The phrase 'creative minority' comes from the English historian Arnold Toynbee, who stressed the significance of small,

---

[27] Clements and Bullivant, *Catholics in Contemporary Britain*, 62–3.

[28] Christian Smith, *American Evangelicalism: Embattled and Thriving* (Chicago, IL: Chicago University Press, 1998).

[29] See, e.g., Anna Strhan, *Aliens and Strangers? Struggle for Coherence in the Everyday Lives of Evangelicals* (Oxford: Oxford University Press, 2015); and Sadek Hamid, *Sufis, Salafis and Islamists: The Contested Ground of British Islamic Activism* (London: I. B. Tauris, 2016). For a number of interesting studies of church growth, across a range of denominations, see also David Goodhew (ed.), *Church Growth in Britain: 1980 to the Present* (Farnham: Ashgate, 2012).

[30] José P. Coutinho, Brian Conway, and Siniša Zrinščak, 'Special issue—Highly Religious Young Catholics', *Sociology Compass* 17/7 (2023), e13118.

[31] Luca Bossi, Loris Botto, Roberta Ricucci, 'Between Research and Revival: Emerging Trends among Highly Religious Young Catholics in Italy', *Sociology Compass* 17/7 (2023), 1–19; Katherine Dugan, *Millennial Missionaries: How a Group of Young Catholics is Trying to Make Catholicism Cool* (New York: Oxford University Press, 2019); Tricia Rivera, 'Young Catholic Women Favour Tradition Over their Older Parishioners' *The Australian*, 14 September 2014, <https://www.theaustralian.com.au/nation/young-catholic-women-favour-tradition-over-their-older-parishioners/news-story/8c9d06cbb1319a67c195632e666f0b25>; Philippa Martyr, 'Let's Ask Youth Why They Stay, Not Why They Go', *Catholic Weekly*, 14 June 2023, <https://www.catholicweekly.com.au/philippa-martyr-lets-ask-why-youth-stay-not-why-they-go/>.

countercultural groups as drivers of social, cultural, and spiritual progress at key moments of history.[32] Beginning in the 1980s, the then-Cardinal Ratzinger began using the term, initially to describe the 'new ecclesial movements', which he saw as real signs of hope in the turbulent years following Vatican II: 'The faith was reawakening precisely among the young, who embraced it without ifs, ands, or buts, without escape hatches and loopholes, and who experienced it in its totality as a precious, life-giving gift'.[33] This chimed with a key idea of Ratzinger's (neo-)evangelistic thinking, which he had been speaking and writing about since the 1950s. Put very simply, he predicted that large-scale secularisation would, after a long period of hardship and decline for the Church – 'reduced in size, diminished in social prestige', and 'no longer… able to inhabit many of the edifices she built in prosperity' (sound familiar?) – ultimately lead to 'a fresh blossoming': 'When the trial of this sifting is past, a great power will flow from a more spiritualised and simplified Church'.[34] This is a theme he returned to periodically during his papacy. For example, speaking to journalists in 2009: 'I would say that usually it is creative minorities who determine the future, and in this regard the Catholic Church must understand that she

---

[32] This paragraph is adapted from Stephen Bullivant, 'Ratzinger and Secularization', in Tracey Rowland and Francesca Murphy (eds), *The Oxford Handbook of Joseph Ratzinger* (Oxford: Oxford University Press, 2024; *forthcoming*). On the whole topic of creative minorities in the theology of Ratzinger/Benedict XVI, consult *The Benedict Proposal: Church as Creative Minority in the Thought of Pope Benedict XVI* (Eugene, OR: Pickwick Publications, 2020). For Toynbee's own usage, see, e.g., Arnold J. Toynbee, *A Study in History: Abridgement of Volumes I-VI*, ed. D. C. Somervell (New York: Dell, 1965), 275.

[33] Joseph Ratzinger, 'The Theological Locus of Ecclesial Movements', trans. Adrian Walker, *Communio* 25 (1998), 480–501, 481.

[34] Joseph Ratzinger, 'What Will the Church Look Like in 2000?', in *Faith and the Future* (San Francisco, CA: Ignatius Press, [1969] 2009). See also Joseph Ratzinger, 'The New Pagans and the Church' (1958), trans. Kenneth Baker, <https://www.hprweb.com/2017/01/the-new-pagans-and-the-church/>.

is a creative minority who has a heritage of values that are not things of the past, but a very lively and relevant reality'.[35]

Note that Ratzinger's 'creative minorities' are, to a significant extent, a direct by-product of secularisation.[36] More broadly, the kinds of strong Catholic groups we will be highlighting in this book are not evidence that secularisation is not happening – or rather, has not for the most part already *happened* – after all. Rather, precisely because religion has 'declined steeply in power, popularity, and plausibility'[37] in Britain overall, then those who are left must necessarily be pretty committed. And so too, of course, must a good number of the friends they make at Mass, CathSoc, Youth 2000, or the Chartres pilgrimage.

Immigration

British Catholicism has another strong suit when it comes to having a guaranteed future – and one that it has been playing for a good while. For much of the past two centuries, the Church here has been continually topped up by successive waves of immigrants. The Irish are the most well-known: at the nineteenth-century high point, the 1861 Census recorded 805,000 Irish-born residents, from a total British population of some 26 million. Numbers have ebbed and flowed over the decades, with large numbers arriving after the Second World War. These peaked at 950,000 in the 1971 Census (albeit from a much higher overall population of 54 million). Growing secularisation in Ireland, as indeed among the Anglo-Irish diaspora, rather reduces Ireland's future prospects for bolstering British

---

[35] Benedict XVI, 'Interview of the Holy Father Benedict XVI during the Flight to the Czech Republic', 26 September 2009, <https://www.vatican.va/content/benedict-xvi/en/speeches/2009/september/documents/hf_ben-xvi_spe_20090926_interview.html>.

[36] Cf. Steve Bruce, 'Secularization and Church Growth in the United Kingdom', *Journal of Religion in Europe* 6/3 (2013), 273–96.

[37] Steve Bruce and David Voas, 'Secularization Vindicated', *Religions* 14/3, 1–13, 1.

parishes.[38] Although that said, Ireland is still among the more religious countries in Western Europe, including among young adults.[39]

Ireland is far from the only major contributor to British parishes, however. Following the Second World War, large numbers from Central and Eastern Europe – a combination of former 'Free' Allied ex-servicemen and their families, and displaced persons unwilling or unable to return to their now-Communist homelands – settled in Britain. These included perhaps 130,000 Poles, 35,000 Ukrainians, plus smaller (but locally significant) groups of Hungarians, Slovaks, and Lithuanians. Due to labour shortages, many others from elsewhere in Europe followed them, often staying for good. Beginning in the 1950s and 1960s, moreover, significant numbers of Catholics began arriving from the Commonwealth, not least from West Africa (e.g., Ghana, Nigeria, Ivory Coast, Sierra Leone) and India (both directly, and via East African countries such as Kenya and Uganda). These Indian Catholics, in turn, comprise distinct linguistic and liturgical groups. Our Malayalam-speaking Syro-Malabars are just one of those we will meet in these pages.[40] Immigration from many other, non-European and non-Commonwealth countries – ranging from Lebanon to Brazil to the Philippines – is relevant here too.

To focus on the present, the Catholic Church in Britain as a whole justifies the term 'superdiverse'.[41] Around 14% of British

---

[38] For two recent treatments of Irish secularisation, see Hugh Turpin, *Unholy Catholic Ireland: Religious Hypocrisy, Secular Morality, and Irish Irreligion* (Stanford, CA: Stanford University Press, 2022); and Derek Scally, *The Best Catholics in the World: The Irish, the Church and the End of a Special Relationship* (London: Penguin, 2022).

[39] Stephen Bullivant, *Europe's Young Adults and Religion: Findings from the European Social Survey (2014–16) to inform the 2018 Synod of Bishops* (Benedict XVI Centre for Religion and Society; Institut Catholique de Paris, 2018), 9.

[40] Eleanor Nesbitt, 'South Asian Christians in the UK', in Knut A. Jacobsen and Selva J. Raj (eds), *South Asian Christian Diaspora: Invisible Diaspora in Europe and North America* (Farnham, 2008), 17–38.

[41] Cf. Steven Vertovec, 'Super-Diversity and Its Implications', *Ethnic and Racial Studies* 30/6 (2007), 1024–54; and Marian Burchardt and Irene Becci, 'Religion and Superdiversity: An Introduction', *New Diversities* 18/1 (2016), 1–7.

Catholics were born elsewhere (i.e., are first-generation immigrants), with most of them from somewhere in Europe.[42] This should come as no surprise. In addition to those mentioned in the previous paragraph, there were very significant inflows during the period between 2004, when six majority Catholic countries (Poland, Malta, Hungary, Slovakia, Lithuania, and Slovenia) were among the ten who joined the European Union, and 2020, when Britain became the first country to leave it. Post-Brexit, those already here could apply to remain. As of summer 2023, either 'settled' (i.e., permanent) or 'pre-settled' (for five years, but able to re-apply for settled status thereafter) status had been granted to, among others, 1.12 million Poles, 600,000 Italians, 440,000 Portuguese (including a significant contingent of Indians from Goa, who are entitled to Portuguese citizenship[43]), 380,000 Spaniards, 280,000 Lithuanians, 160,000 Hungarians, 120,000 Slovaks. Add to all this, following the outbreak of war in February 2022, new arrivals from non-EU Ukraine – joining the significant community already here (see chapter three).[44] Naturally, not all of these will be Catholics, and of those that are, not all will be practising. (This is obvious enough, if there are only 592,000 at Mass, including all the native Britons too, on a typical Sunday.) But many are, as is abundantly clear from Catholic parishes and schools.

---

[42] Clements and Bullivant, *Catholics in Contemporary Britain*, 27.

[43] Joanna P. Coelho, 'Diaspora, Nationality, and the Goan Catholics in England', *Indian Journal of Research* 4/12 (2015), 11–13; Joanna P. Coelho, 'Citizenship and Nationality: The Dynamic "Home" of Goan Catholics in Swindon, England', in Ajaya K. Sahoo (ed.), *Mapping Indian Diaspora: Contestations and Representations* (New Delhi: Rawat Publications, 2017), 31–52.

[44] These are based on the most recently available Home Office figures, as of September 2023. See 'EU Settlement Scheme quarterly statistics, June 2023', <https://www.gov.uk/government/statistics/eu-settlement-scheme-quarterly-statistics-june-2023/eu-settlement-scheme-quarterly-statistics-june-2023#data-tables>; and 'Statistics on Ukrainians in the UK', <https://www.gov.uk/government/statistics/immigration-system-statistics-year-ending-june-2023/statistics-on-ukrainians-in-the-uk>.

In many parts of the country, however, it is non-European migration that's the critical factor in parish vitality. The 2019 survey found that only 2% of British Catholics were born in Asia or Africa. This is very likely an undercount, due to the difficulties of sampling relatively small subgroups, with attendant margins of error. (According to the 2021 Census, for example, the UK as a whole has 155,000 Filipino-born residents alone.[45]) Even if the actual figure is several percent larger, then they, their children, and (in some cases by now) their grandchildren are still likely over-represented in terms of actual church involvement. Of course, a person's perception of all this will greatly depend on where they normally attend Mass. There are plenty of parishes where this won't be evident at all, and plenty of others where it will be abundantly so. It is often especially clear at the younger end of the spectrum: i.e., the kids from the parish school who are actually present at Mass on a regular basis, and/or are involved in such things as altar serving, are often disproportionately those from British Asian (especially Indian or Filipino) or African families. Nor is this only or mainly a London phenomenon, though it is certainly true that London's Catholic churches, like those of other denominations, are clear beneficiaries of immigration.[46]

---

[45] Office for National Statistics, 'The changing picture of long-term international migration, England and Wales: Census 2021', <*https://www.ons.gov.uk/peoplepopulationandcommunity/ populationandmigration/internationalmigration/articles/thechangingpictureoflongterm internationalmigrationenglandandwales/census2021*>.

[46] E.g., Clare Watkins, 'Les défis des inculturations, de la mission inversée et des Communautés: Réflexions à partir de l'expérience multiculturelle de l'Église catholique en Grande-Bretagne' (// 'Challenges of Inculturations, 'Reverse Mission' and Community/ ies: Reflections from the Multi-cultural Experience of the Catholic Church in Britain'), *Revue Lumen Vitae* 77 (2023/4), 418–33.
  On London's relative religiousness, see Paul Bickley and Nathan Mladin, *Religious London: Faith in Global City* (London: Theos, 2020); and David Goodhew and Anthony-Paul Cooper (eds), *The Desecularisation of the City: London's Churches, 1980 to the Present* (Abingdon: Routledge, 2019).

Pastorally and evangelistically speaking, relying on sustained levels of immigration to keep numbers up might seem a little like 'cheating'. Certainly, it is something that few other longstanding British denominations can realistically benefit from, and goes a good way to explaining why the Catholic Church is doing *comparatively* well on many pastoral indicators. In truth though, immigration is not some magic solution to church decline. And indeed, the fact that Mass attendance has been steadily declining over the past decades *despite* large and constant inflows from dozens of much-more-religious-than-us countries suggests that there is a great deal of work to be done here. Evidently, very large numbers of these Catholic immigrants are not present in Catholic parishes. And even among those who are, it is certain that a large proportion of their British-born children become effectively assimilated into the non-practising, non-believing, native norm. In short, the Church needs to do a better job with the immigrants it gets, not least in preserving more of their (relative) religious strength unto the second and third generations. And working out quite how to do that ought to be a large part of the Church's pastoral strategy.

After Secularisation?

Before proceeding, the book's title perhaps needs a little explanation. We mean it in two important senses. The first, and most basic, one is simply that *secularisation* is a process. There is a trend in recent scholarship to use the term 'late secularisation' to describe a socio-cultural condition, which Britain has now entered, marked by 'a combination of a largely formally secular society and an active-involvement-in-organised-religion rate of less than 10 percent'.[47] Either, however, this is conceived as some kind of endpoint of the secularisation process, or else 'late secularisation' is the final stage of the country's secularising, and *then* we reach its endpoint. This endpoint is best termed 'secularity' or rather

---

[47] Bruce, 'Late Secularization', 14.

'secularised-ness', i.e., the point at which secularisation has run its course, and all that is to be secularised has been secularised. Logically speaking, secular-*isation* can't keep going on for ever (short of some Zeno's paradox-style situation, at least).

So the question remains, *after secularisation*, what is, or will be, the state of the Catholic Church (or any other religious body) in Britain? After all, mainstream secularisation theorists don't typically envisage the endpoint as there being *no* religion whatsoever, just that what little is left of it will be socially marginal, having 'declined steeply in power, popularity, and plausibility'.[48] Perhaps British religion's power, popularity, and plausibility has bottomed out already. Perhaps it still has a good way to go. But it cannot *keep on* declining steeply for ever more.

As mentioned above, the suggestion that the Catholic Church, specifically, will decline down to zero, or anything close to it, is simply not plausible. So it makes sense to think about what position the Church will be in when it has declined as far as it's going to – and therefore, about what the Church should be doing *now* to ensure that that ultimate low-point is as high as possible. And it also makes sense to think about what the Church will or should do from then onwards. It is not quite true that the *only* way is up, at least not for any sustained period. Perhaps the Church will hold more or less steady. Perhaps it will rise a little, then decline, then rise a little again. But then again, perhaps it *will* start, if slowly at first, to grow steadily again. 'Up' is, if not a guarantee, then at least an option.

Our second sense of 'after secularisation' relates to the creative minority effect discussed earlier. Secularisation does not happen uniformly in societies, and since it largely proceeds generationally (with each new generation being significantly less religious, on average, than the previous one), then it is clearly the case that the world inhabited by young adults is towards the more secularised

---

[48] Bruce and Voas, 'Secularization Vindicated', 1.

end. Indeed, if the present period is indeed one of 'late secularisation', then the youngest cohorts' experience must be one of 'latest secularisation'. Even if Britain as a whole has some more secularising to do, then the young adult milieu ought by now to be about as secularised as possible. Hence there is a sense in which our close-knit groups of deviantly religious swimmers-against-the-stream are doing so 'after secularisation', because their wider social world in which all this is taking place is already more or less at 'peak secularisation'. As we have argued, their very committedness is, in large measure, a side-effect of, and reaction to, their highly secularised environment.

That, at least, is a large part of the (mostly implicit) argument of the book. While it is not a book *only* about young adult Catholics – indeed, a striking feature of several of our case studies is precisely their multigenerational nature – they naturally feature heavily. It is, after all, a book about the present and future of British Catholicism. Today's young adults, and their current and future children, are critical to both.

Note: This book has three authors, who are jointly responsible for the whole. Each of us has been the 'main drafter' of different chapters, and no doubt some of our individual authorial voices and styles will be evident to readers trained in historical-critical exegesis. If this means that the tone shifts a little from chapter to chapter, then so be it. On stylistic grounds, we prefer that to seeking a bland stylistic middle-ground that sounds like none of us.

We will also be using the 'ethnographic I' in relating some of our fieldwork experiences, as in the above account of AFCM's 'Second Saturday' convention. This seems better to us on stylistic grounds rather than either using the third person, or using cumbersome phrases such as 'one of us'. However, since our positionality and perspectives on things will naturally differ, we identify which 'I' it is in a footnote.

1. Parishes

'Christianity has died many times and risen again; for it had a God who knew the way out of the grave.'[1] From the tales compiled in this book a renewed Paschal Mystery emerges, a contemporary dying and rising of Christ's Body, lived out in the twenty-first century British Catholic Church. Nowhere is this dying and rising more apparent than in the Catholic parish. While other types of Catholic community in this book are new, emerging freshly for sociological and missiological reasons unique to the Church in this time and place, the Catholic parish system is a universal, centuries-old institution. While the parish as an individual geography of people, or the 'presence of the Church in a given territory',[2] originates from the earliest beginnings of Christianity,[3] it was in the sixth century that the term 'parish' became more uniform and tied to territory. Only after the Council of Trent were parish boundaries strictly defined.[4]

Forms adopted by the Church for the spread of the Gospel are historically conditioned and not themselves unchangeable. Indeed, in 2020, the Congregation for the Clergy recognised this in its Instruction on the parish: 'the current Parish model no longer adequately corresponds to the many expectations of the faithful, especially when one considers the multiplicity of community types

---

[1] G K Chesterton, *The Everlasting Man* (London: Hodder & Stoughton, 1925), 290.
[2] Pope Francis, *Evangelii Gaudium*, 28.
[3] St Paul refers to first-century house churches (cf. Romans 16, 3–5).
[4] Tricia Bruce, *Parish and Place: Making Room for Diversity in the American Catholic Church* (New York: Oxford University Press, 2017), 14.

in existence today.'[5] Might there be a case for admitting that the parish system is no longer fit for the evangelisation of the modern world, and that new structures for mission should be pursued?[6] Certainly, untold numbers of religious orders have arisen to serve the Church's mission at particular moments in history, before later dwindling and disappearing, all the while others are arising in their place. (This is something we also see in Britain today.) Might a similar fate lie in store for parishes?

Yet successive popes have indicated that the parish system is of a different order. Pope St John Paul II reflected that, notwithstanding the adaptations to which the parish is called, 'it nevertheless remains an indispensable organism of primary importance in the visible structure of the Church.'[7] Pope Benedict XVI likewise affirmed that 'the parish is a beacon that radiates the light of the faith and thus responds to the deepest and truest desires of the human heart, giving meaning and hope to the lives of individuals and families.'[8] And Pope Francis declared that the parish 'is a community of communities, a sanctuary where the thirsty come to drink in the midst of their journey, and a centre of constant missionary outreach', even claiming that the new expressions of life within the Church (small

---

[5] Congregation for the Clergy, *The Pastoral Conversion of the Parish Community in the Service of the Evangelising Mission of the Church*, 20 July 2020, 16, <https://press.vatican.va/content/salastampa/en/bollettino/pubblico/2020/07/20/200720a.html>.

[6] Broadly analogous debates have been going on in the Church of England, which currently has over 12,000 (!) parishes, for much longer. See, for example, David Berry, *Structures for the Church: Reshaping the Christian Mission to Our Ancient Western Nations* (Malton: Gilead Books, 2008); and Andrew Davison and Alison Milbank, *For the Parish: A Critique of Fresh Expressions* (London: SCM Press, 2010); Andrew Rumsey, *Parish: An Anglican Theology of Place* (London: SCM Press, 2017); and Alison Milbank, *The Once and Future Parish* (London: SCM Press, 2023).

[7] John Paul II, 'Discourse to Participants at the Plenary of the Congregation for the Clergy' (20 October 1984), 3–4, <https://www.vatican.va/content/john-paul-ii/it/speeches/1984/october/documents/hf_jp-ii_spe_19841020_plenaria-congregazione-clero.html> (in Italian).

[8] Benedict XVI, 'Homily during the Pastoral Visit to Our Lady Star of Evangelisation Parish of Rome' (10 December 2006), <https://www.vatican.va/content/benedict-xvi/en/homilies/2006/documents/hf_ben-xvi_hom_20061210_star-evangelization.html>.

communities, movements and other forms of association) should be integrated into 'the rich reality of the local parish', to prevent them from 'becoming nomads without roots'.[9]

Yet all three popes recognise the adaptation needed by the parish in a post-Christian context. Unless the parish demonstrates its 'great flexibility', its ability to assume 'quite different contours depending on the openness and missionary creativity of the pastor and the community', and an agile 'self-renewal and constant adaptivity', sociological forces will brutally prove it 'outdated'.[10]

One of the most significant shifts, proposed by the 2020 Instruction, is from the parish's focus on 'geographical' to 'existential' territory: 'increased mobility and the digital culture have expanded the confines of existence,'[11] it asserts, and, 'the Parish territory is no longer a geographical space only, but also the context in which people express their lives in terms of relationships, reciprocal service, and ancient traditions... [A]ny pastoral action that is limited to the territory of the Parish is outdated, which is something the parishioners themselves observe when their Parish appears to be more interested in preserving a nostalgia of former times as opposed to looking to the future with courage.'[12]

And yet the geographical is not completely abandoned: an abiding characteristic of the parish is still 'its rootedness at the centre of where people live from day to day.' In the post-Christian era, then, there is a curious balance to be achieved between geographical 'rootedness' and existential meaningfulness.

The dying and rising of the Catholic parish, then, is one of metamorphosis: a deep rediscovery of its original purpose, and the

---

[9] *Evangelii Gaudium*, 28–9.
[10] Ibid., 28–9.
[11] 'The Pastoral Conversion of the Parish Community', 8.
[12] Ibid., 16.

creative, missionary adaptation of forms, structures, and methods to serve this purpose.

An Evolving 'Archipelago' of British Parishes

As we explore the metamorphosing of Britain's parishes, a helpful image might be an archipelago of interconnected islands. If we think back even as recently as the turn of the millennium, when typical British Mass attendance was 1,264,000, this archipelago of parishes was vast. Imagine thousands of 'islands', each a canonical parish with church building(s), priest(s), and laity. Over twenty years later, the landscape of this archipelago has changed: hundreds of these 'islands' are now submerged under rising waters of secularism. They are half-forgotten in the neighbourhoods in which they had once been integrated. There are greater distances from one island to the next. Some are becoming perilously small with rising tides, while others grow larger as they keep the tides at bay through missionary outreach, immigration, or through accumulating Catholics from further geographic distances. Today, the 'typical Sunday' population of these islands is less than half what it was a mere quarter-decade ago (with 2022 attendance at c. 594,000). The 'islands' belonging to this beleaguered archipelago are now few at just 2,533 canonical parishes and decreasing with every passing year.[13]

It is certainly a bleak picture and one that would make any reasonable person cry out for the Church to cease closing parishes. Yet, counterintuitively, diocesan restructuring of parishes can in fact precisely be part of the 'missionary creativity' and 'constant adaptivity' required for the 'resurrection' of parishes in the post-Christian era. We would be unlikely to find one diocese in Britain that, if not already restructuring, is not seriously planning it. One diocese we spoke to is

---

[13] This number is true of December 2023. Total numbers of parishes are not recorded nationally, and given the extensive restructuring underway, this number is likely to change frequently.

restructuring from 111 parishes to 52 in the next two years. Another is reducing from 87 down to 25. While restructuring in itself is not enough to prevent the rising sea-levels, it is – paradoxically – needed in order to give some islands and their inhabitants the best chance, not only of survival, but of becoming beacons to those drowning in dangerous waters. One episcopal vicar with responsibility for restructuring in his diocese told us,

> We have an ambitious pastoral plan for the diocese which, in order to focus on mission, involves a radical restructuring of parishes. We will [apply missionary principles for the newly formed parishes] in terms of vision casting, leadership models and structures.

Certainly, as the wisest dioceses are recognising, the most efficient restructuring in the world is worth nothing if not simultaneously accompanied by cultural change, and the new 'missionary creativity' spoken of in *Evangelii Gaudium*. So, what missionary creativity is already bearing fruit among British parishes? How might parish 'islands' ensure their continued existence in the British archipelago ten years from now? And what learnings might newly amalgamated parishes take on board if they are to avoid being lost to history beneath the crashing waves of secularism that have swamped neighbouring parishes?

Parishes as Island 'Sanctuaries'

Ania[14] is a blonde-haired Polish woman in her thirties who found herself teaching at a Catholic school in west London. Little did she know, but an encounter at this school would prove to be a bridge for her onto the 'island' of St Elizabeth of Portugal parish in Richmond. Having been brought up culturally Catholic in Poland

---

[14] Names given to parishioners in this chapter are pseudonyms; the real names of parish priests and staff members are used with their permission.

and later Ireland, Ania found herself taking a gap-year to travel the world. Looking back, she can see that she was seeking God. 'I became an explorer,' she says, 'looking for [God] in science, philosophy, and travel.'

Her seeking took her to India and a ten-day meditation course. 'Sitting in silence, stillness, and faith for that long gave me a powerful experience and I became determined to learn more.' Several yoga courses later and having volunteered in a meditation centre for six months, Ania says she 'became disillusioned with the hyper-individualistic me-and-my-enlightenment approach.' She stopped actively searching: 'I was busy and had little time and energy to indulge spiritual seeking, especially given how disappointing it was.'

Increasingly, she became more interested in social justice and reaching those in society who are marginalised. But even this area of her search led to disappointment: 'over time I found myself again disillusioned with the hypocrisy and self-righteous methods used… Again, I found myself in a place where I sought goodness, community and connection but found to be self-serving and alienating.'

It was when she found herself sitting in the back of a Catholic school classroom marking books, half-listening to two young Catholic women speak to the students about God's love, that something changed.

> When they began to sing the song, I immediately felt a rush over me and knew God was there. I thought, 'Wow, these girls know how to pray!' I was really taken aback by this experience because until then I had assumed Catholicism was a bit of a dead branch but there they were, and there he was…

Speaking to the school chaplain, she ended up being connected into St Elizabeth's parish and a programme they run called 'Catholicism 101'.

> I got a Bible and went into a period of intense research because I knew I missed something important… Going to confession, attending Mass, Adoration and developing a prayer life helped me understand and experience God's love… All this happened around Easter when I was 33 and it felt like my own resurrection into life.

She adds, 'I cannot understate my own surprise to have come full circle… Becoming a member of [St Elizabeth's] parish has been a blessing in my life.'

St Elizabeth of Portugal parish proved to be an 'island' that provided the meaning, belonging, and relationship with God that Ania had searched the world for; for her it was 'a sanctuary,' in the words of *Evangelii Gaudium* 28, 'where the thirsty come to drink in the midst of their journey.' Ania is by no means the only young adult who has found answers to her search at St Elizabeth's. Since it began its intentional journey towards becoming 'mission-oriented' in 2016, over 500 people have taken part in Alpha courses in the parish's attractively refurbished crypt, adorned with informative screens, cosy seating nooks, and fairy-lights. While overall attendance at the parish has not grown (owing to the pandemic effect), parishioner engagement has deepened remarkably. In 2016, when parish priest Fr Stephen Langridge arrived at the parish, a Gallup ME25 survey ranked parishioner engagement at 10%.[15] Repeating the survey every two years since has revealed a growth in engagement to 36%, a high percentage relative to Catholic parishes globally.

Two other London parishes are also seeing impressive signs of health and, indeed, numerical growth. In 2023 and bucking trends of the pandemic, St Bede's in Clapham Park reported its highest

---

[15] The survey is 'a tool that helps church leaders measure and improve the engagement and spiritual health of their faith community.' See <https://store.gallup.com/p/en-gb/10299/faith-member-engagement-(me%3Csup%3E25%3C%2Fsup%3E)-survey-program>.

average Mass attendance in ten years. It even featured in the *Evening Standard* recently, thanks to its regular Latin Masses that are very popular with young adults (see chapter five).[16] Likewise, St Patrick's in Soho reported a 40% increase in the five years to 2023.

Why are these three London parishes reporting such health and vitality while others are flailing? The answer to this question is multi-faceted. It is important to acknowledge that London's population is young, growing, immigrant and transient: the sociological realities of the city's Catholic parishes are therefore quite unique, incomparable to the rest of the country.[17] Yet trends in these three thriving Catholic parishes point to an important emerging reality that can be seen to varying degrees in other parishes across Britain, too.

We can outline two dimensions to this emerging reality: change in Catholics' behaviour, and how parishes are responding to it.

First, let's consider the change taking place in Catholics' behaviour, trends both spotlighted and accelerated by the pandemic. The growth in the three London parishes confirms the intuition of the 2020 Instruction on the parish that the importance of 'geographic' territory is waning to the advantage of 'existential' territory. All three parishes exhibit signs of transfer growth, that is, where Catholics transfer their attendance from one parish to another. The pandemic period was a time of much adjustment for Catholics: significant numbers fell away from the practice of their faith, while those who remained became more discerning about

---

[16] Emily Phillips, 'Holier than Thou: The Rise of Gen Z Catholicism', *Evening Standard*, 4 February 2024, <https://www.standard.co.uk/culture/holier-than-thou-the-rise-of-gen-z-catholicism-b1136795.html>.

[17] London has the highest rate of Mass-going among Britain's Catholics. In 2019, 41% said they attended weekly or more, compared to a national average of 30%. See Ben Clements and Stephen Bullivant, *Catholics in Contemporary Britain: Faith, Society, Politics* (Oxford: Oxford University Press, 2022), 47–8. On London's (comparatively) high religiosity in general, see David Goodhew and Anthony-Paul Cooper (eds), *The Descularisation of the City: London's Churches, 1980 to the Present* (Abingdon: Routledge, 2019); Paul Bickley and Nathan Mladin, *Religious London: Faith in a Global City* (London: Theos, 2020).

what was important to them in a parish 'in terms of relationships, reciprocal service, and ancient traditions' in the words of the 2020 Instruction. In other words, the pandemic hastened choice as a determining factor in the lived practice of Catholics, replacing, one could argue, cultural habit.

We can put this another way: there appears to be a growing trend of people choosing which parish to attend based on reasons other than pure geography.[18] This trend is an interesting one because voluntary association is traditionally associated with a Protestant congregation mentality, yet it is undeniably becoming a feature of Catholics' lived practice. Catholics in London are choosing St Elizabeth's for its Alpha courses and young adult community, St Bede's for its traditional liturgy, music and catechesis,[19] and St Patrick's for its work with the homeless and Adoration.[20] The cultural importance of individual choice and authenticity in the post-Christian era has made an indelible imprint on the practice of Catholicism. Christian Smith and colleagues sum it up well: 'it is by choosing a product, a mate, a lifestyle, or an identity

---

[18] In the 2019 Catholics in Britain survey, 15% of weekly Mass-goers said that they most frequently attended Mass outside of their own parish church. However, this proportion is likely to be (much) higher among younger demographics, and those in major cities, such as London, with a large number of parishes within striking distance. In addition to the three already mentioned, we know of many thriving parish churches – Sacred Heart, Wimbledon; Immaculate Conception, Farm Street; the Brompton Oratory; Our Lady of the Rosary, Haverstock Hill – which attract congregations from beyond their (geographical, if not 'existential') parish boundaries due to offering something distinctive, and doing it well. There is also, of course, a significant number of Catholics who travel out-of-parish for Masses in languages other English, whether modern foreign ones or Latin. These are the focus of chapters three and five.

[19] St Bede's website states, 'St Bede's is a traditional Catholic parish known for its excellence in liturgy, in music and in catechetical formation (the passing on of the faith).' See <https://stbedesclaphampark.org.uk>.

[20] Fr Alexander Sherbrooke, parish priest at St Patrick's, reports that the parish has 'about 120 volunteers who help with our work with the homeless, we probably have about sixty people who regularly engage with Eucharistic adoration… And we've probably got about forty people who are engaged with works of evangelisation. On a weekly basis we probably feed about 300.'

that makes it one's very own, personal, special, and meaningful – not 'merely' something one inherits or assumes.'[21] As in the rest of their lives, Catholics are applying this principle, too, to the practice of their religion.

The second dimension to this emerging reality is, of course, how Catholic parishes are responding. St Elizabeth's, St Bede's, and St Patrick's seem to have caught something of the *Zeitgeist* of (especially younger) twenty-first century Catholics' practice and are growing accordingly. But what precisely are they getting right?

First, they each seem to understand themselves as serving an 'existential territory'. We might say that parishes can operate either according to a 'geographic' or an 'existential' mindset. Sociologist Tricia Bruce summarises the 'geographic' mindset:

> In the language of organisations, territorial parishes act as generalist organisations aiming to serve all in a heterogenous market. They target the middle, accessing the highest number of 'customers' (parishioners).[22]

The 'geographic' mindset is deeply ingrained in Catholic parishes and dioceses. In market terms, it is a mindset that sees parishes supplying blanket, seamless provision of the Catholic 'product' across an entire geography where every postcode is covered. This mentality works in the 'Christendom'[23] reality of a stable, homogenous religious society. But in a post-Christian, heterogeneous, pluralist society, the 'geographic' mindset attempts the impossible. In the words of sociologists Rodney

---

[21] Christian Smith, Michael Emerson, Sally Gallagher, Paul Kennedy, and David Sikkink, *American Evangelicalism: Embattled and Thriving* (Chicago: University of Chicago Press, 1998), 103.

[22] T. Bruce, *Parish and Place*, 7.

[23] Cf. Sherry Weddell, *Forming Intentional Disciples: The Path to Knowing and Following Jesus*, rev. edn (Huntington, IN: Our Sunday Visitor, 2022).

Stark and Laurence Iannaccone, it aims to satisfy all religious preferences via one 'religious firm',[24] or, in Bruce's words, a 'generalist organisation'. 'The more heterogeneous a population,' she says, 'the more difficult it is to appeal to all through a generalist organisation'.[25]

'Targeting the middle' – with a 'geographic' mindset – in fact fails to meet genuine spiritual need. Stark and Iannaccone argue that, 'where people are not confronted with a range of efficient religious suppliers, low levels of religious consumption exist'. What results is 'an unattractive product, badly marketed, within a highly regulated and distorted religious economy'.[26]

While applying such market terminology to the Church is controversial and somewhat jarring,[27] their analysis offers an explanation as to why Catholic parishes are dismally failing in the context of 'late secularisation'.[28] Stories like Ania's leave us in no doubt that spiritual needs are abundant; yet parishes that operate according to the 'geographic' mindset are perfectly designed to fail to meet these needs. If individual choice now increasingly motivates Catholics' behaviour, the majority of parishes have not yet caught up. In Bruce's words, 'Territory and fixity battle choice and movement. Parish evokes propinquity, but behaviour prompts trans-localism. Parishes stay. Catholics move.'[29]

---

[24] Rodney Stark and Laurence Iannaccone, 'A Supply-Side Reinterpretation of the "Secularization" of Europe', *Journal for the Scientific Study of Religion* 33/3 (1994), 230–52, at 241.

[25] T. Bruce, *Parish and Place*, 7.

[26] Stark and Iannaccone, 'A Supply-Side Reinterpretation', 241, 232.

[27] Though see the following for more jarring examples: Stephen Bullivant, 'Economic Models of Church Life: Three 'Nudges' towards Better Behaviour', *Theology* 125/1 (2022), 27–34; and Stephen Bullivant, 'Mass Markets and the "Liturgical Long Tail"', *Antiphon* 26/1 (2022), 1–25.

[28] Steve Bruce, 'Late Secularization and Religion as Alien', *Open Theology* 1 (2014), 13–23.

[29] T. Bruce, *Parish and Place*, 66.

What is the hallmark, then, of a parish that has embraced its 'existential' territory? St Elizabeth's, St Bede's and St Patrick's have intuitively grasped the attraction to postmodern seekers of 'distinctiveness.'

Christian Smith's sociological research of thriving religious subcultures discovered that, in the context of pluralism, distinctiveness from *other* groups or subcultures – knowing 'who they are in large measure by knowing who they are not'[30] – is not a threat to religious vitality but is rather an indicator of success. When Ania's drive for meaning and belonging was satisfied, it was in the context of a community that sustained a distinctive identity to which she could belong. Strong religious subcultures like St Elizabeth's actually grow stronger in the context of pluralism, which provides 'a diversity and abundance of ideological and cultural outgroups' against which to comprehend one's identity.[31] It is this instinct that has enabled St Bede's and St Patrick's, likewise, to develop 'existential territory' mindsets and strong subcultures. They know that Catholics and seekers alike are being driven by 'choice', not by postcode, and will move to find a community that satisfies their desire for, in Smith's words, 'morally-orienting collective identity.'

Catholic parishes that maintain a 'geographic' mindset, on the other hand, aim more passively to serve all within their territory, complacent in the hope that the baptised in their locality are drawn magnetically to their local parish for their sacramental and pastoral needs. Yet in failing to build strong, attractive subcultures, sufficiently distinctive from what is on offer in wider, secular society, they miss the opportunity to answer the spiritual seeking of the postmodern person for whom the Catholic Church could be an 'island sanctuary.' When parishes fail to adapt, the results are tragic all round: seekers remain lost in the flood of secularity, unable to

---

[30] Smith et al., *American Evangelicalism*, 91.
[31] Ibid., 97.

discover parish 'islands', while parishes become smaller and smaller, and eventually are submerged.

It is not only London parishes that are developing distinctive subcultures and existential mindsets. In this chapter, we will show how other adapting, British parishes are exhibiting similar signs: an outsider focus; new forms of community, faith transmission, and leadership; and a growing confidence to reach out.

Outsider Focus: Reaching the Lost

The tragic scenario painted above is one of seekers and parishes alike, drowning in secular waters, unable to reach one other. Certainly, the ability of a parish to go out to find those who are searching is a sign, among other things, of an 'existential' mindset which we will explore below. Yet, what happens when seekers – non-religious and otherwise – arrive at the parish? What do they find? Westminster Cathedral reported having to turn worshippers away on Good Friday 2024 as the building reached its 3000-person capacity.[32] While this is indeed a very encouraging sign of spiritual interest, it also raises the question of what a seeker might experience when they reach the doors of a Catholic parish. Are we ready for them?

People arrive at Catholic churches for myriad reasons. Of those who come through the doors at St Patrick's, Fr Alexander says, 'Many have been drawn by Adoration, many have had conversations with people on the street through street evangelisation.'

Sophie, a young woman in her twenties, describes the night she first entered the doors of St Elizabeth's: 'That night I walked the streets around the church in loops, delaying the moment, staring up at the brilliant full moon. Surely, I thought, to sit and soak up the light of the moon would be far better than [going to church].' She eventually

---

[32] Thomas Colsy, 'Westminster Cathedral forced to turn people away due to unprecedented numbers attending Easter Triduum', *Catholic Herald*, 2 April 2024, <https://catholicherald.co.uk/westminster-cathedral-forced-to-turn-people-away-due-to-surge-of-attendees-for-easter-triduum/>.

arrived for the Alpha course: 'before I had a chance to pretend my being there was a mistake, I was downstairs, glass of wine in hand, eating delicious food and making easy conversation with nice people.'

'It's so lovely to see you again!' may not be words one would expect to hear walking into a Catholic church, but they are ones that have meant a lot to Lucy, another woman who has recently been received into the Church at St Elizabeth's: 'They say it to me every week and it's honestly the loveliest thing, it just makes me feel so welcome. Don't stand outside, go in, you will be so welcome there. It's just so full of love.'[33] Greg, a young man who became a Catholic at the same time as Lucy, agrees. 'I'm thinking of how we need to leave everything that is how we conform in life at the door, leaving the secular world outside – just drop it at the door – and then come on in. The welcome I experienced was amazing and it made me feel at home right from day one.'

At another parish, a young mother, Joyce, describes how she longed to go into her local Catholic church. She would walk past, wanting to go in but not sure if she would be welcome. She eventually built up the courage to walk through the front doors of the church. 'I had to summon every ounce of courage to open the door, because I wanted to be there. [My daughter] needed to be there, too.' Initially, she stood in the foyer of the church throughout the entire Sunday Mass, not daring to go into the church.

For Catholics whose weekly paths to Sunday Mass are familiar and well-trodden, the feelings of anxiety and trepidation at crossing the threshold, described by Sophie and Joyce, may seem unimaginable. But the parishes of these two young women have been successful at adopting an 'outsider mentality': imagining the vulnerability involved in making one's way into a Catholic church,

---

[33] Contrast this with the testimonies of many non-practising Catholics who stress the lack of welcome in parishes as a large part of their alienation: Stephen Bullivant, Catherine Knowles, Hannah Vaughan-Spruce, and Bernadette Durcan, *Why Catholics Leave, What They Miss, and How They Might Return* (Mahwah, NJ: Paulist Press, 2019), 12–18.

they have creatively resolved to lower the discomfort barrier. An 'outsider-focussed' parish realises they exist for the sake of those who do not yet belong and considers signage, the language they use, and the experience of walking through the doors.

Signs of spiritual hunger in the culture suggest that this might be energy well-spent by parishes determined not to continue shrinking. High profile interest in Christianity, and even conversions, among those who would class themselves as 'nones', alongside popular commentary from intellectuals such as historian Tom Holland and psychologist Jordan Peterson, among others, show the reinsertion of Christianity into (the fringes of) public discourse. A common thread seems to be the search for assurance in the midst of growing disillusionment and anxiety. The Christian commentator, Justin Brierley, author of *The Surprising Rebirth of Belief in God*, says,

> I still see the values we have inherited from the Christian story bubbling away subconsciously in our moral instincts for compassion, equality and freedom. I still see people searching for justice, beauty and meaning in their lives, often in quasi–religious ways. The Christian story has not been buried so deep that it cannot surface again in our country. I see hopeful signs that it will.[34]

Sophie's testimony resonates with Brierley's instinct. She says,

> I'd explored spirituality previously, had felt that lightning bolt start of God's love at a dark hour, had meditated, prayed, read sacred texts. I was nervous of someone trying to bundle up and bind my infinite, boundary-defying God in the name of organised religion. And yet, I had a feeling Catholicism might offer me a way to know God in a deeper, more intimate way.

---

[34] 'Is the UK a Christian Country?', *Theos*, 6 September 2023, <https://www.theosthinktank.co.uk/comment/2023/09/06/is-the-uk-a-christian-country>.

She is among the ten young adults under 35 who became Catholic at St Elizabeth's in the space of two years. 61% of those who class themselves as having 'no religion' were brought up as Christians (at least to some degree), with 11% lapsed Catholics. On a scale of 0-10 where 0 is 'not at all religious' and 10 is 'very religious', 15.3% remarkably ranked themselves between 7-10. 10.6% said they attended religious services at least once a month or more frequently. 9% said they prayed at least once a month, with 4% saying they prayed every day.[35] In other words, the probability that 'nones' cross the threshold of our local Catholic parish on an average Sunday is higher than we may have thought. St Elizabeth's experience is that a cheery 'It's so lovely to see you [again]!' goes a long way.

Certainly, those entering the Church are increasingly coming from unexpected places, and often with complicated backgrounds. At a parish in Luton, Fr Brendan Seery tells a story about a man called Craig. 'This guy just turned up one day,' the church was open, and Craig was sitting in one of the pews. He told Fr Brendan he instantly 'felt at home when he came to the church.' He was in a programme getting clean from narcotics and knew he couldn't do it on his own, he needed God. Now Craig is 'on fire with the Spirit' and has also brought a friend, Derek, to the faith. 'If you saw them, you'd probably run a mile because, they have tattoos, they're big guys, they look scary if you don't know them, but they are soft as anything – they are incredible.' Derek was one of the six adults baptised at Easter 2023.

One Welsh parish priest reports a young man requesting help with an issue of demonic oppression. The priest went to bless his house, taking him a Bible to read. 'After a while he came to church,' reports the priest, 'sat at the back at Mass, then asked more

---

[35] All statistics from the British Social Attitudes survey, as analysed in Stephen Bullivant, *The "No Religion" Population of Britain*, (London: Benedict XVI Centre, 2017), <https://www.stmarys.ac.uk/research/centres/benedict-xvi/docs/2017-may-no-religion-report.pdf>.

about the Catholic faith. He had purchased images of the saints to strengthen his defence against the attacks. Then he asked to join our 'Journey in Faith' group. I believe that the work of the Holy Spirit can be seen here, one step at a time.' Eventually this man, too, joined the Catholic Church.

Regardless of how they end up in our churches, what is critical to any 'none' who makes it past the threshold is the discovery of community, and it is to this second sign of an adapting parish that we will now turn.

New Forms of Parish Life: Community

Digging into the archives of one Lancashire parish, in the years between 1930 and 1950, one discovers a parish community quite unimaginable to Catholics in Britain today. The picture that emerges is of an intensely religiously and socially close-knit community.

There is the extravagant crowning of the May Queen (a First Communion girl) and her retinue each year; the fully-attended 7:30am daily Masses; sodalities such as the Guild of the Blessed Sacrament (women who clean and care for the altar), the Children of Mary (girls from 16 years old), and the Guild of St Agnes (girls from 11). All take their turns to pray in front of the Blessed Sacrament during the Forty Hours devotion, the Children of Mary wearing blue cloaks and white veils and praying in twos. There are Blessed Sacrament processions, senior and junior youth groups, the Catholic Men's 'club' (i.e., a bar) that never opens until after Mass, Benediction, and devotions are finished, and whose accounts in 1954 show a large amount of money spent on Mass intentions. It would be 'unthinkable to enrol in an evening class on a Thursday because that was Benediction night.' A parish Amateur Operatic Society formed in 1958 produced high quality Gilbert and Sullivan productions every year.

In a fairly homogenous Christian society, the Catholic parish played a powerful identity-affirming role for the historically beleaguered minority Catholic population. The parish served as an identity-legitimiser until the modernisation of the 1960s when Christianity was increasingly rejected and the Catholic parish as identity-legitimiser weakened. The 1960s and 1970s saw the Catholic parish increasingly become 'a kind of service station where the people had their religious and spiritual needs satisfied', in the words of American sociologist Jay Dolan.[36] Sociologist Michael Hornsby-Smith comments that, while British parishioners may have 'still retained a few religious "reflexes"' their 'everyday conduct in the sexual, ethical, political, or educational domains' is less and less guided by the Church.[37] The religious lives of Catholics has become disentwined from their social and cultural lives. 'Enrolling in an evening class on Thursday' becomes increasingly conceivable, whether it is Benediction night or not. If you belong to an Amateur Operatic Society, it is unlikely to be connected to your Catholic parish. And normal Catholic behaviour involves attending Mass on a Sunday and little else.

Fast-forward another sixty years, and the Catholic parishes that are successfully standing firm against the tides of secularism are those who have rediscovered the role of community in forming distinctive subcultures. While anonymity clearly holds an attraction for the curious (the Good Friday numbers at Westminster Cathedral attest to this), community that entwines the religious, social, and cultural seems to be increasingly sought.

Richard, a Scottish man in his forties, brought up Catholic but later lapsed, reflects that, 'I lost sight of the fact that the church was community.' Gradually being brought back to his childhood faith over many years, he signed up for an Alpha course at his local Catholic parish in Erskine, not far from Glasgow. He recalls,

---

[36] Jay P. Dolan, *The American Catholic Experience: A History from Colonial Times to the Present* (Garden City, NY: Doubleday, 1985), 397.

[37] Michael Hornsby-Smith, *The Changing Parish: A Study of Parishes, Priests, and Parishioners after Vatican II* (London: Routledge, 1989), 60.

I became aware as the course progressed that a deeper understanding of Christianity would never come from solitary study and reflection alone, but rather via dialogue and through sharing personal experience and listening to the experience of others. Genuinely, I think I have learned substantially more and gained much greater insight and understanding from the weekly discussions in Alpha, than I did through any of the multitude of books I've read or lecture series I've followed. I received a different form of insight. One that I couldn't just get on my own, staying in my own head. A lot of the blind spots and hesitations I had about Christianity were addressed, and from this my faith is substantially more robust than it was.

For Sophie, too, community was an indispensable route into the Church. 'Mass seemed too intimidating, too different,' she says, but joining a course at the parish seemed less of a high bar. 'I loved our small group discussions. We had really good, genuine, totally non-judgemental, heartfelt, sometimes hilarious, sometimes emotional conversations. Through these conversations, I started to see the Church, this community of people all striving to better reflect God's love.'

The parish in which Richard returned to his faith is St Bernadette and St John Bosco, led by Fr David Boyd. It is another example of a parish pursuing vitality and growth in a secular environment. Over the last several years, Fr David and his parishioners have worked hard to reverse the decades-engrained behaviour of disengagement outside Sunday Mass. 'We measure the percentage of people who attend Mass but who are also actively involved in some form of ministry, discipleship group or connect group', Fr David explains. Their efforts have paid off. While in 2020, roughly 20% of Mass attendees engaged in other activities, by 2023, the figure increased to 45%. Building a close-knit community has enabled someone like Richard to rediscover faith 'through sharing personal experience and listening to the experience of others.'

Fr Stephen's experience at St Elizabeth's is similar. When asked what is attracting people to the parish, he replies, 'It's a question we ask at our new parishioner events and the answer is nearly always the same: community. Our online registration form has a section which people can tick to support us financially, volunteer to help, enquire about a house group or about Alpha. About two thirds of respondents express an interest in house groups.'

It is an intriguing finding which suggests that the religious 'service-station' of the 80s no longer satisfies spiritual need. Catholics who sustain the 'service-station' level of engagement will likely fall away; yet those who, like Ania, Sophie, Richard, Lucy, and Greg, entwine their social and cultural lives into the parish, increase their probability of remaining strongly engaged.

New Forms of Parish Life: Faith Transmission

Like community, the handing-on of the faith has suffered from the disentwining of the religious, social, and cultural domains in the British Catholic parish since the 1960s. Mary is a catechist who has volunteered for twenty years in a north London parish. She shares that in the academic year 2022-3, 'only half of the families preparing their children for First Holy Communion were in Mass on any given weekend. Today we see only a fraction of them regularly coming to Mass.' She expresses a widespread reality across Catholic parishes where the social and cultural lives of Catholic families are disengaged from their religious lives. In an oppressively secular milieu where, nevertheless, the family continues to cherish the cultural threads that tie them to Catholicism, religious participation is kept minimal.

The traditional sacramental programme undertaken at milestone moments of a Catholic's life made sense in the context of the 1950s Lancashire parish described above. In such a parish, a young person was embedded in a web of relationships, experiences and events that nourished and formed their identity and faith. But in twenty-first century Britain, this web of relationships is threadbare, often non-existent. In such a context, the sacramental programme undertaken by the young person immersed – not in a distinctive Catholic subculture but in a culture hostile to religion – is like a single drop of water in stifling heat: it very soon evaporates.

Yet, most British parishes labour extensively to maintain such programmes. As their islands become smaller, and their inhabitants fewer, they (maddeningly?) use their shrinking resources to maintain functions that no longer make sense without the wider subculture in which they were embedded.

Mary's parish came to a radical decision that enough was enough in 2023. 'It was clear we couldn't keep doing the same thing and expecting different results,' she said. 'We decided to stop running a sacramental programme for children in school Year 3 and to instead offer family catechesis sessions – Growing in Faith Together (GIFT).' The decision reflects a trend among a growing number of parishes that not only sees that a different form of sacramental preparation is needed, but that a new form offers an opportunity to rebuild afresh a distinctively strong subculture. At GIFT, the whole family takes part once a month, not just children in a particular school year. Parents-only sessions follow online. 'Families now meet individually with our priest to discern together where they are on their faith journey and when both we and they think that the time is right [they] take the next step,' says Mary.

Parishes from north London to Runcorn, and from Erskine to Brighton, are following a similar approach. While few demographic similarities exist between such places, the experiences of the Catholic parishes are very resonant. Fr Peter Wright, parish priest at St Maximilian Kolbe, Runcorn, says, 'Our programmes were a total failure.' His team, too, now takes a more individualised approach. 'Each [family] is linked with one catechist who then accompanies them throughout the journey; true friendship and support develops. It takes as long as it takes for the parents to feel comfortable in being practising Catholics who are growing in faith; then and only then do we speak of sacramental celebrations.'

Canon Kieron O'Brien, the parish priest at St Joseph's in Brighton, agrees. His parish decided to employ a lay person dedicated solely to family ministry. 'We are working towards a model of life-long formation where sacraments are celebrated when individuals are ready rather than at fixed points, between which there is nothing.' St Joseph's, too, is seeing the need to integrate the social into the religious experience of families: 'We are creating new opportunities for families to worship, pray and have fun, such as enhanced Liturgy of the Word for Children and regular "Messy Church".'

These parishes are realising that big, one-off sacramental celebrations like First Communion Masses can unwittingly reinforce a culture of segmenting the religious dimension of life: the family's sights are on the 'one big day' before they get back to their non-practising normal. Anne-Marie, a catechist at Fr David Boyd's parish in Erskine, said, 'Our starting point was the realisation that for many families the day of First Communion is maybe the last day for a long time. We knew that this could not continue.' But her parish, like the others, now attempt to help the family normalise the religious by integrating it into everyday life.

Concurring with this different approach to celebrating first sacraments, Mary from the North London parish says, 'We no longer have a couple of weekends when large numbers of children come together to celebrate their first Holy Communion.' The family come to the sacrament of Reconciliation together, and 'any Sunday Mass can be a day for First Holy Communion.'

All parishes report encouraging results. Before introducing the new model in Erskine, Anne-Marie says, 'we had very few children attending Mass. Now we regularly get around forty children between the two parishes.' She shares,

> Young people are engaged in the life of the parish spiritually and in social action. Families are having fun together, chatting together and participating in reflective activities after Mass. Something surprising is that the young people are powerful witnesses already. They encourage one another, they remind each other, they tell the story of their faith at school and in the community.

Mary agrees that, 'it is so rewarding to see families talking together about their faith and growing together in love and community.'

Both Mary and Anne-Marie reflect on what has changed. They agree that initiating the changes was 'challenging'; Anne-Marie admitting to being 'apprehensive' beforehand. 'We are far from perfect,' she says, 'and we have many opportunities lying ahead to continue to rely on the Holy Spirit and to find ways to meet the needs of our community.' Mary shares that her own experience of discipleship motivates her work with the families at the North London parish. Years ago, attending a parish mission, she experienced a change in her heart:

> I knew Jesus loved me and wanted me. I came to understand that it didn't matter what mess I may have made of my life in the past – if I was contrite and determined to change and follow him – Jesus would accept me just as I am and would use me for his glory. This was the start of a joyful journey of conversion which eventually took me to seek reception into the Catholic Church.

She knows there is deep spiritual fulfilment on offer to every loosely-connected family seeking sacraments, and that is why she is passionate about the changes they are making. 'I want everyone to know the joy I have experienced in my faith journey,' she says. 'I know we cannot keep doing what we have been doing if we want to renew the church.'

Of course, 'distinctiveness' is essential to the parish that is adapting within the post-Christian culture, and styles of handing on the faith differ widely. At St Bede's, groups like the Guild of St Clare, St Rita's Women's Group, St Joseph's Men's Group, and the Sodality of Our Lady for girls aged 8-18 bear more than passing resemblance to the 1950s life of the Lancashire parish. Yet it is a positive example of a parish rediscovering the value of, and recreating – hundreds of miles south and seven decades later – a strong, distinctive community where parishioners' social and cultural lives are integrated into the spiritual.

Georgia Clarke, youth minister at St Elizabeth's, is building such a distinctive subculture among teenagers in Richmond. Shifting their preparation for the sacrament of Confirmation in a similar approach to First Communion in the parishes described above, teenagers at St Elizabeth's are invited to receive Confirmation in a similar way. A weekly youth group and monthly socials create an environment in which their faith grows until they and the parish discern they are ready. After celebrating the sacrament, they are invited into a three-year discipleship process. Starting the process with just six teenagers in 2020, four years later they are ministering to roughly forty teenagers on a weekly basis and seeing an 80% retention rate after Confirmation. Georgia said,

> In September 2023, we asked [the teenagers] if attending youth group had increased their daily prayer life and how often they attended Mass/sacraments. 75% said that since they joined youth group they pray more often and 62.5% said they go to Confession more often than before.

Georgia reports whole families returning to Mass since their child's involvement in the youth group, families who have begun a practice of family prayer, and young people inviting their friends to the parish.

> One young person felt such an overwhelming presence of God through prayer ministry, he said that it was just pure love and he wished everyone in the world might also experience the same. He said it was enough to last him a lifetime.

St Elizabeth's has used the three-year experience to foster a strong, parish discipleship subculture. One 14-year-old, commenting on the one-to-one mentoring she receives said, 'I've learned how to get close to God in every little or big thing I do. [Youth group is] a very loving, understanding, and welcoming place.' She adds that Sunday socials are the context in which this growth in faith occurs. 'The Sunday socials are also an opportunity to get away from schoolwork or any worrying thoughts,' she says. Another 15-year-old, affirming the integral role of the social dimension, adds, 'Occasionally we just hang out by the river or complete treasure hunts in town, but lately we've been taking the train or bus to bowling alleys, escape rooms, and crazy golf centres, which are extremely fun.'

While the style of youth gatherings at St Elizabeth's and St Bede's might differ, the emphasis on handing on orthodox teaching in the Catholic faith is identical. One young adult at St Elizabeth's describes their experience of receiving weekly teaching in the Faith that led them to become Catholic:

> I think it was a number of things that each week I kept falling in love with. For example, when we did the session on Mary I was like 'Wow! That's amazing! Mary's amazing!' Then when we did the session on the Eucharist, I thought, 'Of course, that makes sense,

I want that!' Each week, I came back from these classes just really excited and falling in love with what I was learning. It was an overwhelming feeling of joy and wanting to go back to the faith every single week, every single Sunday. I realised that I was never going to turn my back on it again, so why wasn't I becoming Catholic?

The more flexible, individualised approach to faith formation, undertaken in the context of community, is summed up well by parish priest of Most Holy Redeemer in Essex, Fr Dan Mason. His parish realised they needed to create what they call a 'discipleship pathway' to help seekers and parishioners alike continually move forward in their relationship with Christ. Urging every parishioner to consider what their next step in discipleship might be, Fr Dan explains, 'it will mean being prepared to leave your comfort zone and to try something new.' Recognising that there is no 'one-size-fits-all' for any individual, the parish communicates multiple different offerings and 'ways in' to faith. They want to grow in numbers as well as faith: their ambitious goal is to increase by 10% every year until 2026.

New Forms of Parish Life: Leadership

These stories from parishes adapting in the face of secularisation demonstrate much innovation, creativity, and openness to change. It is clear that reaching the spiritually seeking – who are present in great numbers in our local neighbourhoods – *is* possible, but that new methods are required. New methods are inextricably coupled with new modes of leadership. It is unlikely that any parish priest we have encountered so far would have seen the same fruitfulness had they sustained the leadership model for which seminary trained them.

Fr David Boyd, whose Scottish parish we met above, describes the moment when he reached breaking point in his priesthood. Newly arrived at two merged parishes, Fr David had been 'run ragged' for months, trying to meet the expectations of parishioners who wanted the same level of service from one priest they had previously received from two. He felt increasingly like a 'sacrament machine'. Then on one fateful weekend, he celebrated two Baptisms where both families made it clear they would not be coming back to church. This was the moment where Fr David describes feeling 'destroyed'. Leaving for a holiday in Spain, he says he was close to emotionally 'checking out' of his priestly vocation.

On arriving in Spain, he was bewildered on opening his Kindle to find at the top of his downloaded books, *Divine Renovation: Bringing your Parish from Maintenance to Mission*, by Fr James Mallon.[38] To this day, he cannot explain how it ended up there: his plan had been to read only fiction. Curiously beginning to read, he grew in astonishment at Fr James's own parallel experiences in a parish hundreds of miles away in Nova Scotia, and his diagnosis of how parishes needed to change to meet the needs of the twenty-first century. Much of the diagnosis and the blueprint for change suggested by Fr James is shared by the parishes we have witnessed in this chapter, fruitfully adapting to mission in a post-Christian era.

Returning to Scotland with new hope and energy, Fr David distributed the book to his closest lay collaborators. These five lay people eventually formed a team around him to share responsibility for the day-to-day leadership of the parishes. He no longer makes isolated decisions or leads alone, and he says that this group of people "saved his priesthood."

---

[38] James Mallon, *Divine Renovation: Bringing your Parish from Maintenance to Mission* (New London, CT: Twenty-Third Publications, 2014). Many of the parishes featured in this chapter have found inspiration and coaching from Divine Renovation, a global parish renewal ministry founded in 2018. Over the six years of the ministry's operation in the UK, parishes from Aberdeen to Essex, from Cumbria to Birmingham, and from London to Newport are employing the three principles of parish renewal – the power of the Holy Spirit, the primacy of evangelisation, and the best of leadership principles – and are beginning to see fruits. See more at <www.divinerenovation.org>.

If a parish 'island' is not only going to maintain itself, but also to build itself as a 'sanctuary' for those seeking and as a launch point for the rescue mission, many extra hands are needed. Helping all parishioners see themselves as leaders of others has become vital for Fr Stephen Pritchard, parish priest at Our Lady of the Assumption, in Gateacre, Liverpool. Gathering all those involved in any ministry or service role within his parish one June day in 2023 was the beginning of a new approach where parishioners began training to see themselves not only as 'island dwellers' but as part of the rescue mission. Ministry and small group leaders have been trained to spot the gifts in others, inviting them to grow in these gifts. Groups are being encouraged to grow in an outward-focussed approach with specific goals in mind, and in an approach that maximises the use of each person's gifts: 'What more could we accomplish by drawing on each other's strengths?' They receive training in leading meetings that 'eliminate frustration and create engagement and passion,' and in working through and resolving conflict in a healthy way. Fr Stephen invites groups of six or seven parishioners for a meal at a time to reflect on the growing leadership culture in the parish.

Where there is growing activity and new people crossing the threshold, the role of the weekly homily takes on a new significance as an evangelisation and leadership tool for the parish priest. Fr David shares how another leadership shift for him has been how much time he spends on preaching preparation:

> Now I spend about eight hours a week preparing, in prayer, researching and putting together the homily. I have… had to challenge myself in the use of technical language or insider words or concepts. I have had to focus on the assumption that many people will not know what these words mean. As a result, I have many people, including many who attended Mass regularly, say that they now clearly understand.

As a leader of leaders, the role of the parish priest subtly shifts towards equipping the laity for the rescue mission.

A Growing Confidence to Reach Out

Leaving the parish 'island' and going in pursuit of the lost is the fifth and final sign exhibited by parishes bearing new life, and it is in many ways the most important: the sign towards which all the others are ordered. When Fr Stephen Pritchard gathered his Gateacre parishioners in June 2023, he would not have guessed what might result from his attempts to foster a leadership culture in his parish. Just under one year later, at Easter 2024, his parish appeared on local television as they performed a dramatic, musical representation of the Stations of the Cross in the local shopping centre. Crowds gathered alongside BBC North West news, as one hundred parishioners performed the Belle Vale Passion. One parishioner taking part and interviewed on the news clip, said,

> I was never going to get involved in it. I'm not doing that in the shopping centre. No chance. But I've just been swept along with it, and something's been calling me to do it.

The transformation of parishioners from secluded 'island-dwellers' into confident, public missionaries is at the heart of the metamorphosing of Catholic parishes that we have been exploring. A desire was kindled in the hearts of parishioners in June 2023 to 'do church inside out', and months later they found themselves witnessing very publicly in the local shopping centre.

Certainly, plenty of Catholic parishes around Britain have a strong tradition of serving deprived local neighbourhoods. St Joseph's in Brighton uses its buildings creatively by fostering partnerships with local charities, including a 'pay-as-you-feel' community café, which helps 'to provide social cohesion in a deprived area', according to Canon Kieron O'Brien. Fr Peter Wright, in

Runcorn, describing his parish neighbourhood as one of 'acute social deprivation', remarks how generous his parishioners, often poor themselves, are to the local food bank:

> When the gifts are dropped off each week the collectors always comment that 'the Catholics' are the most generous in the town. At Christmas and Easter, I could cry when I see the expensive boxes of chocolates or eggs that are left for the food bank. Through the blinds I can see some of the poorest folk being the most generous as they, Ninja-like, drop off goods and money.

Yet offering material help alone is not 'distinctive' enough for a Catholic subculture. Those feeling adrift in contemporary society are seeking not only material, but predominantly spiritual help. The parishes showing signs of new life couple explicit witness to the faith with their social outreach. One homeless man in Richmond shared his experience of St Elizabeth's night shelter:

> Alcohol [was] my crutch and as time went on my drinking got worse. I'd have these chronic relapses. In 2018 I lost my job and was in and out of hospital. By the end of October, I was in a critical state: I'd run out of money, was homeless and drunk. Two of my friends committed suicide. When I arrived at the night shelter I could barely walk. I was a mess. At the night shelter I felt safe, and I started to get a sense of community. I was embraced by people who had faith and who loved us... The shelter brings community, so loneliness is no longer a trigger for self-destruction. At the night shelter we all got to know each other: guests and volunteers. I began to be able to help people. I'm lucky to be alive. St Elizabeth's helped me rediscover what friendship is. I'm really grateful to every single one of the volunteers. Their love has had a humanising effect. I'm amazed at how warm and kind and trusting people are to sit down with homeless people and love them.

His experience is a fruit of the outward-focussed faith of St Elizabeth's parishioners which is gradually becoming a normative part of the culture. One retired parishioner tells her story of witnessing to her faith with a stranger. Sitting on the bus one autumn day, she was prompted to engage with a young woman beside her who began sharing her difficulties. The parishioner asked whether she had been brought up in a religion, and shared how important faith was in her own experience of suffering. The parishioner said later,

> This experience of sharing my faith is new for me. I became a Catholic thirty years ago… [It was only] a couple of years ago that I realised we are all called to be disciples and that it is my role, along with every baptised Catholic, to share the Gospel. Evangelisation isn't just for priests and church-workers. Before that I wouldn't normally talk about my faith but… being part of the parish community has given me the courage I needed to do it. The best thing about that conversation on the bus it that it didn't feel strange at all… it felt totally natural.

The purpose of the leadership training in the Liverpool parish, and of the 'discipleship pathway' in the Essex parish, is to form parishioners from the early beginnings of a relationship with God through to confident apostolic mission. This was the journey that parishioner Tom Storey underwent. Returning to Mass for the first time after many years following his father's death, Tom met a man in his seventies named Bill. Bill was friendly and welcoming, making an impact on Tom. 'I was drawn back by him… the faith that he had… it was just very beaming through him.'

Gradually Tom got more involved in church. One day, a couple that Tom met in an online parish group said to him that they saw a love of Jesus beaming through him that was drawing them back each week. It was at that moment that he saw the transformation that God had been working in his life. Now he does not feel right if his day does not start with his morning prayer time and scripture reading. He meets with a spiritual director regularly, is involved in ministry at the parish and reads at Mass.

But more than that, he finds himself talking about Jesus often. Every Saturday morning you can spot him on the streets of Richmond with his chocolate brown dog. But he isn't just taking Rory for a walk – he is part of a homeless ministry. Walking in a group of between four and six other parishioners he talks with men and women who are on the streets and brings them tea and sandwiches. Faith has changed the way he sees himself: it starts 'aligning all you're thinking about. You start thinking completely differently about everything and your priorities change.'

'Thinking completely differently about everything' sums up well the metamorphosing of Catholic parishes we have seen in these pages. While holding on to what is unchanging, such as doctrine and liturgy, these parishes have been faithfully reinventing themselves – becoming more outward-focussed, developing new forms of life in terms of community, faith transmission, and leadership, and being proactive in reaching the lost.

Conclusion

Greg, one of the young adults received into the Church in recent years at St Elizabeth's, described drifting away from his faith: 'Without even realising I was drifting. I think many people have this experience. I got caught up in work, I got caught up in London social life – it's so easy to do.' He described what this drifting was like:

> The kind of drifting I suppose like at the beach, when you get in the ocean and then realise that your parents are miles away in the other direction, even though it felt like you'd only been in the water ten minutes!

By the time he realised how far he'd drifted, he said, 'I felt I wasn't good enough to come back.' Yet he was brought along to a course at church and something there held onto him, to the extent that he willingly made a two-hour commute from home each week.

> The people there were incredibly inspiring. It wasn't the 'perfect' world we see today through social media. I think that reality is something I find relatable. Brokenness makes things more beautiful. Meeting people I could connect with in that deeper way, rather than on a materialistic level.

Gradually, he saw that he would be 'welcomed back into the church, back into God's grace and arms', and he knew this would be his home.

Parishes' reinvention and creativity featured in this chapter are not only preventing their own closure – their gradual submersion beneath rising, secular tides – but, more crucially to their fundamental purpose, are reaching those who, like Greg, have drifted without realising it from the shore, or, like other stories we have heard, have become lost in the waves. In the Introduction, we noted that the Church's decline will bottom out at some point, and that any 'bounce back' will largely depend on her willingness to adapt. Learning from some of the parishes featured here might even catalyse a resurgence, as Christianity rises again from its watery grave.

2. Youth Movements and Initiatives

It goes without saying that the experience of youth ministry in most British parishes is not akin to that described in the last chapter at St Elizabeth's, Richmond. The more familiar experience is expressed in the 2022 National Synthesis Document, from the Bishops' Conference of England and Wales, summarising the diocesan phase of the Synod on Synodality.[1] In this synthesis, one of the marginalised groups is listed as young people. The document states,

> Present in almost every submission was the pain in the older generation at the absence of young people from the Church, along with a bewilderment that the means of passing on the faith in a previous generation through family and parish had broken down. The question was often voiced: 'how can we encourage them to come back?' (§62)

Certainly, venture into many a Catholic parish on any given Sunday morning and the grey-haired incumbents of pews likely outnumber those of younger generations. 70% of British young people aged 16-29 are 'nones', compared to 53% in the general population.[2] Yet while young people are notably missing from the

---

[1] CBCEW, 'National Synthesis Document', 22 June 2022, §62, <https://www.cbcew.org.uk/wp-content/uploads/sites/3/2022/06/synod-national-synthesis-england-wales.pdf>.
[2] Stephen Bullivant, *Europe's Young Adults and Religion* (Twickenham: Benedict XVI Centre for Religion and Society), <https://www.stmarys.ac.uk/research/centres/benedict-xvi/docs/2018-mar-europe-young-people-report-eng.pdf>.

parish system explored in the last chapter, this institutional form of the Church does not tell the full story.

John,[3] 29, has been involved with Youth 2000, a Catholic spiritual initiative for young people, since he was 17. It was at a Youth 2000 retreat — a multi-day event centred around the Eucharist, contemporary praise and worship music, and fellowship with other young people — that he says he first encountered God. Through making his first, honest Confession at a Youth 2000 retreat, and through experiencing the healing power and presence of Jesus in the Blessed Sacrament, John says his life changed. He shared:

> Without Youth 2000, I am not sure I would be someone who seeks the Lord every day, seeks His mercy when I fall, and desires to have a heart that aches for people to know themselves and know Jesus.

The consistent presence and prayerful support of many priests and religious brothers have kept him coming back for twelve years. These are men with whom he has shared inspiring conversations and received advice. He adds, 'Youth 2000 has become a place where I serve, grow as a person, have community. It has been a life raft in some of the most difficult times of my life.' He is now discerning a possible vocation to the priesthood.

In contrast to anecdotal experience at the average Catholic parish, our research reveals a rising generation of passionate and committed young Catholics who, like John, while not necessarily receiving faith through traditional routes of transmission (family, parish, school), are emerging with great zeal onto the Catholic scene from other quarters, and indeed, shaping that scene.

---

[3] Names given to young people in this chapter are pseudonyms; the real names of staff members are used with their permission.

In this chapter, we shall use the term 'young people' to refer to those aged between 16 and 29 years old, on occasion referencing teenagers under 16 and young adults in their early thirties.[4] As of 2024, those aged between 12 and 27 are categorised as 'Generation Z' (i.e., born 1997-2012, inclusive), and throughout the chapter, we will also refer to certain recognised traits of 'Gen Z' to shed light on the attitudes and behaviours of young Catholics.[5]

Declining Generations?

In the late 1970s, when John's parents were themselves children or (just) young adults, sociologist Michael Hornsby-Smith conducted a wide-ranging investigation into the state of Catholicism in England and Wales. He discovered that the outlook of Catholics on questions of faith and morals was increasingly indistinguishable from those of the wider population. The impact of the parish becoming 'a kind of service station' – a social reality explored in the last chapter – took its toll on ordinary Catholics' beliefs. Hornsby-Smith termed this, 'a residual form of Catholicism' where tenets

---

[4] There are many ways of defining what is meant by 'young person'. The XV Ordinary General Assembly of the Synod of Bishops that convened for the Synod on 'Young People, the Faith and Vocational Discernment' in 2019 defined "youth" as those who are roughly aged 16 to 29 years old (see <https://www.vatican.va/roman_curia/synod/documents/rc_synod_doc_20181027_doc-final-instrumentum-xvassemblea-giovani_en.html>). However, 'youth' can refer differently depending on context. The United Nations, for statistical purposes, refers to those aged between 15 and 24 as 'youth' (see <https://www.un.org/en/global-issues/youth#:~:text=Who%20Are%20the%20Youth%3F,of%2015%20and%2024%20years>). In the UK, 'youth' more commonly refers only to teenagers (for example, the 2011 governmental national youth policy relates to those aged 13 to 19), while those over 19 might be more commonly termed 'young adults'.

[5] We follow here the categorization by Pew: Michael Dimock, 'Defining Generations: Where Millennials End and Generation Z Begins', *Pew Fact Tank*, 17 January 2019, <www.pewresearch.org/fact-tank/2019/01/17/where-millennials-end-and-generation-z-begins/>. At the same time, we acknowledge that generational categories are not sharply defined and include vast numbers of very diverse people. At the risk of oversimplification, however, they are useful shorthands for thinking about broad differences of age-related culture and outlook.

of Catholic faith were being filtered by most Catholics through their own 'personal interpretative processes'. This 'residual form of Catholicism', he surmised, was due to 'a breakdown in the processes of formal socialisation… processes of trivialisation, conventionality, apathy, convenience, and self-interest, which had eroded and modified the formally prescribed beliefs and practices of Roman Catholicism'.[6] It was John's grandparents' generation that were interviewed by Hornsby-Smith. And even for that generation, the traditional apparatus of faith transmission (family, parish, school) was failing.

Such findings in the late 70s seem now, with hindsight, a prophetic warning of the dilution and decline of Catholicism. Sociologist Steve Bruce holds that, for religion to survive in 'late secularisation',[7] it is necessary 'to produce a shared social product'.[8] A diluted, heterogeneous, individualised faith is difficult, if not impossible, to hand on: 'there is no longer a common stock of knowledge from which shared answers can be drawn'.[9] In other words, if the faith was primarily transmitted through the filter of 'personal interpretation' by the grandparents, parents, teachers, clergy and catechists of the late 70s, it is no wonder that for John this attempted transmission failed. Indeed, the impact of the failure of these methods is clear. In the 29 years from 1990 to 2019, Mass attendance among Catholics in Britain halved from 1.6 to 0.8 million (see Appendix), as hundreds of thousands of Catholics shrugged off any 'residual' Catholicism and succumbed to a 'diluting' of their faith and the magnetic pull of secularity.

---

6   Michael Hornsby-Smith, *Roman Catholic Beliefs in England: Customary Catholicism and Transformations of Religious Authority* (Cambridge: Cambridge University Press, 1991), 219.
7   See Introduction for a brief discussion of this concept.
8   Steve Bruce, 'Late Secularization and Religion as Alien', *Open Theology* 1 (2014), 13–23, 14.
9   Bruce, 'Late Secularization', 15. Elsewhere Bruce writes, 'I cannot see how a shared faith can be created from a low-salience world of pick-and-mix religion' (Steve Bruce, *God is Dead: Secularisation in the West* [Oxford: Blackwell Publishers, 2002], 105).

Certainly, the pull of secularism is strong and pervasive, and the trend among Catholics surveyed by Hornsby-Smith in the late 70s was to camouflage their beliefs with secular cultural outlooks, downplaying the distinctiveness of Catholicism and preferring to blend in. At that time, it was clear that frequent attendance at Mass was much more prevalent among older people (likely John's great-grandparents),[10] who presumably were stronger in resisting the trends to dilution.

One might expect, therefore, that with each generation a general weakening and decline would occur, resulting in a rapidly disappearing religion. Yet John's story indicates that something else is afoot.

Fifty years since Hornsby-Smith interviewed John's grandparents' generation, those who refuse to blend into secular culture are no longer the elderly. As referenced in the Introduction to this book, it is now young Catholics who, by their commitment, stand out more than older ones (those aged 45+). Indeed, 41% of Catholics aged 18–24 – and 45% of those aged 25-34 – attend Mass weekly, compared to 30% of the wider Catholic population. What is more, their commitment is further shown in doctrinal orthodoxy and other indicators of engagement.

Commitment from young Catholics is sustained in small community pockets. One 21-year-old woman affirmed John's experience of Youth 2000 saying, 'I have found a community of people who love me for who I am, and I've found a God that loves me unconditionally.' And university students in Liverpool and Lancaster told us that joining the Young Christian Workers' initiative, Impact!, was faith-sustaining for them. One 19-year-old male said, 'I loved the great camaraderie between everyone.'

---

[10] Michael Hornsby-Smith, *Roman Catholics in England: Studies in Social Structure since the Second World War* (Cambridge: Cambridge University Press, 1987), 45.

And for a 20-year-old female, 'I class the members in the group as my second family!'[11]

Wider secular culture means that identity and belief are now necessarily more strongly married than fifty years ago (why would you tick the 'Catholic' box unless it actually *meant* something?). The normalisation of 'no religion' since Hornsby-Smith's research means that, unlike their parents or grandparents, John's generation has had to *embrace*, rather than downplay, the distinctiveness of their religious faith – or else lose it altogether. Increasingly, 'fuzzy'[12] Catholicism is being eroded from the religious landscape by the dominating forces of secularisation. But rather than a defeat for Catholicism, it in fact signals a growing strength. The young Catholics remaining in the pews might be smaller in number, but they are stronger in energy, commitment, and zeal.

Creative minority effect: Community

In the Introduction, we introduced Pope Benedict XVI's concept of the 'creative minority'. Such minorities are by-products of secularisation that emerge as 'survivor' Catholics grow stronger in commitment and identity. The creative minority effect is vividly identifiable among communities of young, practising British Catholics. While all the organisations and conferences we discuss in this chapter embody the creative minority effect, here, we share glimpses into two such communities, before commenting on the phenomenon in more detail.

★★★

---

[11] These are fascinating insights from young Catholics seeking community outside their family. The Barna survey reports that family is not a major priority for Gen Z. Personal achievement, whether educational or professional (43%), and hobbies and pastimes (42%) are more central to Gen Z's identity than family background / upbringing (34%). See <https://www.barna.com/the-open-generation/>. We have no way of knowing whether these statistics are any different for young Catholics. But our data reveal that young Catholics do seek community, even if outside their family.

[12] Cf. David Voas, 'The Rise and Fall of Fuzzy Fidelity in Europe', *European Sociological Review* 25/2 (2009), 155–68.

YOUTH MOVEMENTS AND INITIATIVES

Hanging out with Dominican Sisters on a week-night might not seem the activity of choice for 17-year-olds. However, according to four teenagers in north-east Scotland, that is precisely how they choose to spend their evening once a fortnight. One young man, who travels thirty minutes to attend the Sisters' Elgin-based youth group, said, 'without the community [the Sisters] bring, it would just be people going to Church. But we go on retreats, have BBQs and things. ... I feel like it's really cemented my faith inside of me.'

Since 2013, four Nashville Dominican Sisters[13] have been steadily building a youth group aimed at secondary school-aged teenagers at their convent in the small Scottish town. Today, roughly fifty young people attend fortnightly. Retreats, conferences, and pilgrimages supplement the regular weeknight gatherings. Following the LifeTeen model,[14] youth group starts with a game setting the theme for the night. 'One fun one we had recently I called the "Davidic Hat Dance",' says Sr Angela Marie. 'This was to introduce a night on King David, and because he "wore" so many different hats as ruler and song-writer, etc., we played a musical-pass-the-hat game, which ended in peals of laughter.' A kerygmatic teaching follows, after which activities are designed to help young people apply the catechesis to their daily lives. 'Then we always end in the chapel with prayer,' Sr Angela Marie says. 'The youth love Adoration the most, so we often end with some praise and worship songs in Adoration. Young people help play instruments and sing, and we guide [them] to respond to God's invitation of love that we

---

[13] The Congregation of St Cecilia, commonly known as the Nashville Dominicans, is a religious institute of religious Sisters located in Nashville, Tennessee. Their primary apostolate is education, and they are present in Scotland at the invitation of Bishop Hugh Gilbert, to develop ministry to young people.

[14] LifeTeen is a youth ministry movement based in the United States that provides parish-based programmes to lead teenagers into deeper relationship with Christ and his Church (see <*www.lifeteen.com*>).

were talking about that night.' For one participant, it is community that keeps him coming:

> I've made so many friends. It's all about being there for each other and having that thing in common, our faith, it's so good to have that support from other people your age. Our parish is an elderly parish; it's still a good community, but having the Sisters makes it more personal, and it's good to be able to ask questions and have that community. What attracts me to youth group is the discussions we have together, ... and to be able to have fun with other Catholics. We keep each other going to youth group, asking each other to come along.

Over the past ten years, the number of young people has grown so much that there are now three youth groups catering for different ages. A third teenage girl tells us, 'Before youth group, I felt that I didn't have a space to talk about my faith freely at school, only about two or three Christian people in my year group. Going to youth group, I got to meet so many people who shared my faith, and I've been able to have these really great, profound discussions about what we believe and things. And it's really, really inspiring to be able to keep looking at my faith.'

'We can all trust each other,' a fourth adds. 'I enjoy the time we spend together talking about our faith whilst also having fun.' The first young man makes a final comment: 'I think going on to university, I'll always have that faith inside of me... It's showed me there are so many people like me who believe the same things as me.'

★★★

Hundreds of miles south, around the same time that the Dominican Sisters were founding the Elgin youth group, another group of Catholic friends were meeting regularly to support each other in their personal faith journeys. They described themselves as young Catholic creatives who loved worshipping Jesus through contemporary praise and worship music and, in their own words, 'wanted to see the world filled with the praises of God.' In 2012, realising that worshipping Jesus just among themselves was no longer enough, they started One Hope Project (or OHP), a worshipping community that wanted to help others do the same. Founders Joe Wells and Pippa Baker say, 'We long to help people in the Church to be inspired and equipped to live out a life of worship to Jesus. Our mission is to encourage fresh expressions of worship in the Catholic Church.'

Since 2018, OHP have led music and worship for over 13,000 young people at events, retreats, and schools across Britain. At many of these events, they not only share music but the Gospel message through teaching and sharing their testimonies. Online, their music has been streamed three million times, while YouTube videos have had 450,000 views.

One young adult who has found a spiritual home in this group said, 'In OHP I found community. A network of young Christian professionals who are passionate about living out a Christian lifestyle – one of loving well, of prayer and of worship in all its forms. We're passionate about bringing people together to encounter God. There is an appetite in today's world to live from a place of gratitude, to look out for each other, to feel part of and play a part in something bigger than yourself. One Hope Project offers an avenue to this and more.'

Responding to demand from young people who sought to be equipped to lead music in their own contexts, including parishes, Joe and Pippa launched the One Hope Project Worship Academy in 2020. The Academy is a six month online worship school that provides formation, teaching, and spiritual mentoring for each student. In the last three years, 51 students have graduated, 74% being under the age of 35. Joe comments, 'We have seen that when people connect their hearts with God in worship this helps them to develop their ongoing relationship with Jesus.'

Young Christians of other traditions are also attracted to the OHP community, and unity with other Christians is an important value for the group. One young evangelical told us, 'OHP has been a real blessing to my faith. I moved back to London in 2015; I didn't have a church family and was nervous about making new Christian friends in a huge city. After getting to know them, I was invited to get involved with all types of OHP activities... As a non-Catholic I have been blessed by getting to know more of my Catholic family and being able to learn about, enjoy and share in parts of Catholic practices. Members of OHP are super inclusive as well, demonstrating significant pastoral care for others despite being located all over the UK! I've made some life-long friends and am so grateful for the gift that OHP has been in my life!'

***

We might be forgiven for thinking there would be little common ground between a group of teenagers in northern Scotland, and a group of young professionals in London. But their comments show that as 'creative minorities' there are abundant similarities. While distinctiveness in religion was dismissed with some embarrassment by the Catholics interviewed by Hornsby-Smith, distinctiveness is precisely what these young Catholics fifty years later seek and what keeps their faith alive. The Elgin youth group acts as a kind of sanctuary for faith where teenagers repeatedly share how crucial it is for them to be with others with the same beliefs. According to one 15-year-old:

> Before coming to youth group, I was a little bit ashamed. That's not the right word, a little embarrassed about being a Christian because it set me apart from other people and it wasn't 'cool.' Since coming to youth group, I've seen that it's more about your

connection with God than anything else. ...Without the youth group, my faith definitely would have died off, and being able to spend time with the Sisters and talk about my faith has allowed me to grow so much and keep it alive.

Embarrassment about faith plays an interesting role here: for earlier generations, embarrassment about their Catholic faith led them to downplay it and blend into the wider culture. Indeed, as the anthropologist Mary Douglas could write as early as 1970: 'Now there is no cause for others to "regard us as odd"... Now the English Catholics are like everyone else.'[15] For the above-quoted 2020s teenager, however, it was embarrassment that drove him to seek out a distinctive subculture – *not* like everyone else – to which he can belong. The sea-change over the course of fifty years is evident.

In line with Steve Bruce's views about how religion can survive in late secularisation, American sociologist Christian Smith, in a study of evangelical Christianity, developed 'subcultural identity theory'. In his view, minorities find their drive for meaning and belonging satisfied only when they can locate themselves within 'social groups (or subcultures) that sustain distinctive, morally orienting collective identities'.[16] Helping to explain why the Elgin teenager seeks 'collective identity' with other young Catholics, Smith asserts that distinctiveness from other groups, far from being a threat to religious vitality, is actually an indicator of strength. Our Scottish teenagers and London young professionals know 'who they are in large measure by knowing who they are not'.[17] Conflict

---

[15] Mary Douglas, *Natural Symbols: Explorations in Cosmology* (London: Routledge [1970] 1996), 44.

[16] Christian Smith, Michael Emerson, Sally Gallagher, Paul Kennedy, and David Sikkink, *American Evangelicalism: Embattled and Thriving* (Chicago: University of Chicago Press, 1998), 103.

[17] Smith et al., *American Evangelicalism*, 91.

with certain out-groups, rather than weakening belief, in fact builds in-group strength. In Everton's words: 'External conflict helps build internal cohesion'.[18] Smith's study of Protestant evangelicals revealed that their sense of being under attack by wider society and culture in fact strengthened their beliefs and commitments.[19]

All of this indicates that the writing was very much on the wall for earlier generations of British Catholics, who shed the distinctiveness that would in fact have sustained their faith. However, does it also suggest that an entrenched, inward-looking subculture is the only way for a creative minority to survive? Is an oppositional posture towards wider society and other subcultures truly necessary?

The experience of the One Hope Project young professionals indicates the opposite. At the heart of their experience has been a desire to share the Gospel with others, and people are attracted by their outward-focussed and inclusive posture. Going further into Smith's research, we discover the evangelistic opportunities available to a distinctive subculture. The meaning and belonging that drive people to find community is at the heart of the postmodern quest: it is a universal search, not exclusive to the self-identified religious person. In Smith's words, 'for all our science, rationality and technology, we moderns are no less the makers, tellers, and believers of stories that make sense of our existence, history and purpose than were our forebears at any other times in human history'.[20] In other words, the postmodern is characterised by a desire to find identity, belonging, and meaning within the context of a subculture, or, according to Smith's metaphor, a 'sacred umbrella'.

---

[18] Sean F. Everton, *Networks and Religion: Ties that Bind, Loose, Build-up, and Tear Down* (Cambridge: Cambridge University Press, 2018), 40.

[19] Smith et al., *American Evangelicalism*, 139.

[20] Christian Smith, *Moral, Believing Animals: Human Personhood and Culture* (New York: Oxford University Press, 2003), 64.

In the not-too distant past, the average Briton's religious outlook was likely to be shaped by a 'sacred canopy', an overarching Christian (i.e., mostly Anglican in England and Wales, mostly Presbyterian in Scotland) culture that offered a vague, and somewhat 'beige',[21] spiritual orientation to life. By now, however, this canopy undeniably lying in tattered fragments, the 2020s person is no less searching for collective meaning. Now, however, such identity is found beneath smaller, yet not less sustaining, 'umbrellas':

> We suggest that, as the old, overarching canopies split apart and their pieces of fabric fell to the ground, many innovative religious actors caught those falling pieces of cloth in the air and, with more than a little ingenuity, remanufactured them into umbrellas. In the pluralistic, modern world, people don't need macro-encompassing sacred cosmos to maintain their religious beliefs. They only need 'sacred umbrellas', small, portable, accessible, relational worlds – religious reference groups – 'under' which their beliefs can make complete sense.[22]

In Elgin, and London, 'small, portable' worlds have been created that are, importantly, 'accessible, relational worlds': open and outward-looking, while not compromising on the distinctiveness that makes them attractive in the first place.

There may be one or two exceptions to the 'sacred umbrella' rule. One 19-year-old from a remote Scottish island commented that there were few Catholics around him as he grew up. He said, 'When I was the only Catholic in my year group, it felt that if anyone asked me about my faith, I had no one to back me up.'

---

[21] Cf. Andrew Greeley, 'A Cloak of Many Colors: The End of Beige Catholicism', *Commonweal*, 9 November 2001, 11–13; Robert Barron, *Bridging the Great Divide: Musings of a Post-liberal, Post-conservative Evangelical Catholic* (Lanham, MD: Sheed & Ward, 2004), 11–21.

[22] Smith et al., *American Evangelicalism*, 106.

Yet, moving to Elgin, he found himself on a pilgrimage with the Dominican Sisters to World Youth Day in Lisbon, Portugal. Speaking about this experience, he observed, 'you're sat, looking at 1.5 million Catholics, and your mind cannot compute it all. It generates a big feeling of not being alone, a lot of security in your faith, and also confidence, to be able to say, "Yes, I'm Catholic"... I feel like I have those 1.5 million Catholics behind me, backing me up, and all the angels and saints.'

His experience indicates that, while distinctive subgroups sustain faith on a day-to-day basis, there is still an important role for a larger, more global, 'canopy' experience, where we discover that our small 'sacred umbrellas' are but subparts of a much larger, if dispersed, patchwork marquee.

An Encounter More Powerful than Anxiety

While distinctive community is one factor that accounts for stronger commitment among young Catholics, to explain the phenomenon by this *alone* would be reductively sociological. On the contrary, the accounts from young people are awash with references to and experiences of the supernatural. A 22-year-old One Hope Project Academy graduate said,

> I cannot tell you how just how much I know the Father's love now. It is the most beautiful and precious thing I have ever experienced, and it's changed me completely. One Hope Project have helped me meet God in worship and it's completely healed me. And I want to share it with the world now.

Such moving accounts are particularly interesting in the context of typical characteristics of Gen Z. A 2022 Barna survey found that an experience of internal pressure characterised young people (56% felt a "pressure to be successful" while 42% felt "a need to be perfect") as well as an experience of anxiety (47% felt "afraid to fail", 51% felt "anxious about important decisions" and 45% felt "uncertain about the future").[23] In other words, for the young people in our research, an experience of prayer or encounter with God seems to be an important refuge from pressure and antidote to anxiety. To dive deeper into this phenomenon, we explore two more groups of young British Catholics.

★★★

One antidote to anxiety is joy, and Julie MacFarlane-Barrow says that this is the whole purpose of the new charity, Generation Hope, she founded with her husband, Magnus:

> It is so important that [young people] know that joy is something they all deserve to experience, that God yearns for them to be truly happy, and that ultimate joy is found in him.

Generation Hope is a fruit of the well-known Scottish charity, Mary's Meals – a charity that provides meals at school for children in the world's poorest communities – also founded by Magnus MacFarlane-Barrow. Witnessing many instances of British young people exposed to the reality of God through their involvement in Mary's Meals, Magnus created a three-day retreat for school groups aged 12-15 to allow them to encounter God's love. Initially hosted at Craig Lodge, Dalmally, 2023 was a milestone year: the first Generation Hope summer camp was hosted at Cairn Brae, Perthshire, for 146 teenagers.

Julie tells how these Our Daily Bread retreats and summer camp are reaching young people with no religious background,

---

[23] See <https://www.barna.com/the-open-generation/>.

including a 12-year-old boy who took part in an Adoration and Reconciliation service. She says:

> After the Adoration service, he said that he felt Jesus say something very specific to him through the Eucharist. When the Gen Hope team visited his school, they found out that he has continued to pray; he keeps rosaries by his bed and has been wanting to get to Mass on Sundays.

At Cairn Brae, young people stay in cosy log cabins beside a picturesque loch. Each day finds them canoeing, ziplining over the loch, water trampolining and tree climbing. After a day of outdoor adventures, they are welcomed into a big tent to listen to the Gospel message from passionate, young adults. They participate in times of worship, Mass, Adoration, and Confession. One 14-year-old boy, hitherto far from the Church, went to Confession: 'The next day he looked physically different and seemed joyful and confident', says Julie. 'When the team visited his school, he was unrecognisable – he truly looked like a different person.'

Following these retreats, prayer groups are starting in schools, young people are undertaking more charitable works on behalf of Mary's Meals (e.g., a group of fifty students fasted on porridge for five days, raising £16,000) and one school even organised a pilgrimage to Medjugorje. Julie comments,

> Young people who are spiritually hungry – without even realising it – are meeting the Lord and encountering him on a personal level. We can't underestimate just how much of a miracle it is every single time one of these kids joins in praise and worship, receives communion, attends prayer ministry, or goes to confession, as everything in the society they are living in, is telling them not just that they don't need God, but that he does not exist. Generation Hope is [telling young people] that they are loved and cared for beyond measure.

A teacher who accompanied the children on the camp reported that parents had been phoning, asking what had happened to their children: they seemed different since attending camp. The teacher said that her students 'seemed happier in themselves, more secure, and like they know that they matter. The young people now meet every week to pray together.' Another teacher said, 'We had a chat with the students and most of them testified that they are more willing to follow Jesus and to be open to letting him use them as vessels.'

Not only are the young people being impacted, but also the teachers themselves. One non-Catholic teacher accompanying the children "started to ask lots of questions about Catholicism and wanted to know... how to pray. When it was time for her group to go out canoeing, [she stayed with a team member to] chat together... for two hours they sat on the bank of the loch and talked about the faith. The next day she said that she had been up all night googling about Catholicism."

★★★

Just as Generation Hope offers a message and experience to young people that counteracts anxiety, Youth 2000 also pierces what can be a stifling lack of transcendence in the culture – and unashamedly tells young people there is something more. A Catholic spiritual initiative that was founded in 1990, it has a strong track record of offering young people a life-giving alternative to the secular culture. 101 priests and consecrated religious attribute their vocation in some part to the work of Youth 2000. Over the last five years, over 2,000 young people have attended their annual summer festival.

At the heart of Youth 2000 events is a Eucharistic healing retreat. A priest, flanked by two altar servers, carries the monstrance holding Jesus in the Blessed Sacrament. Young people quietly come forward, kneeling in a line before him. The priest brings Jesus to each person, and they take hold of the humeral veil, eyes fixed on Christ. Some bury their faces in the veil, others simply gaze at the Lord. Some have tears in their eyes, others have a prayerful intensity. After a few seconds, the priest takes Jesus to the next person. These are momentary encounters but again and again stories are told of lives changing in those few moments:

> I felt God's love and healing in my heart, making my love for him so much stronger. Youth 2000 has changed how I live my life now and I'm completely different to who I was when I first went to a retreat. (Female, 21)
>
> During my first Summer Festival, back in 2016, I was sat in Adoration during the middle of the night, and I realised for the first time that God loved me specifically. I heard His voice speak to me for the first time and, during what was a really difficult time of my life, I felt His peace and consolation. This was a very simple experience but had a very profound and long-lasting impact on my faith. (Female, 26)
>
> It was the gateway into the life of the Church for me. It wasn't a quick fix, but a genuine encounter that left me longing for more when I went home. (Female, 31)

Confession, too, is frequently spoken of as a place of encounter:

> I've had great Confession, personal breakthrough in prayer that I'd not encountered for years, and I've found community that nourishes. (Male, 24)
>
> [The retreat] was my first encounter with God. However, going to Confession changed my heart that night. I then truly encountered God in a way my rational mind couldn't explain during the healing service. I was in tears of joy for hours after this, when I realised how loved and wanted I was by God. (Male, 29)

It is striking how similar these encounter experiences are to those shared by young people ten or more years younger at the Generation Hope camp in Perthshire. Yet, for both, Adoration and Confession are the common places where, in the young people's words, 'encounter' and 'breakthrough' are experienced. Certainly, community is critical, and small groups where young people can speak vulnerably with one another are at the heart of a Youth 2000 event. But even more significant than this seems to be moments of direct contact with God who reveals his love, consolation and presence to a generation burdened by anxieties and pressures. One 15-year-old girl sums it up saying,

> I really felt a sense that God was telling me that He has been with me from the start of my journey, and He is with me now. He was always calling me to His Church, even when I was away from it. In that moment, it was a great consolation.

We cannot neglect to refer to the miraculous, too, when we consider the role of encounter with the supernatural. A 30-year-old woman told of a physical healing she received at Youth 2000:

> I experienced healing in the healing service of my ankle which had been injured and swollen for many years. The swelling completely went, and I was no longer in pain after praying for it in the healing service!

A physical healing was also reported at a One Hope Project Worship Weekend:

> A 25-year-old woman had suffered with rheumatoid arthritis for many years. This caused her pain every day and often meant she couldn't work. Every morning she would have to wake up at 4am to take painkillers. On the Saturday evening of our weekend, we felt prompted to pray for the Lord's healing for anyone

that needed it. She came forward to receive prayer and she testified to experiencing pins and needles all over her body and an instant complete relief of pain. That next morning, she didn't have to take any painkillers, and months on she continues to be completely free of all issues.

Swimming against the Tide: Discipleship and Mentoring

We have noted that it is a community's difference from, rather than similarity to, secular culture that attracts young people to the 'sacred umbrellas' we have been exploring. In contrast to common trends among Catholics fifty years ago, committed young Catholics of the 2020s seek not only belonging but also meaning in a community that does not try to camouflage itself with the wider culture. This has been the experience of Fr Marcus Holden, the parish priest of St Bede's, Clapham Park, that we encountered in chapter one. He, together with Fr Andrew Pinsent, has led Evangelium conferences for young adults since 2008. These three-day, residential conferences offer formation in Catholic faith and spirituality. Over the last fourteen years, 2,000 young adults have attended. When asked what keeps young people coming, Fr Marcus agrees that 'clear teaching which draws from the treasury of the Catholic Tradition' is critical, along with 'beautiful liturgy and experience of worship that leads one to a sense of awe and inspiration', and 'fraternity that gives companionship on the difficult road of faith and encouragement to work together.'

Jack Regan is director of a Catholic youth retreat centre, Castlerigg Manor, in the Lake District. Every year they welcome between 2000 and 3000 teenagers from schools into their retreat programme. Speaking of the outlook of teenagers arriving at Castlerigg he says,

> I'm not seeing the resistance that we got from millennials around the notion of truth and dogma. Millennials could be quite feisty when presented with 'this is truth', whereas Gen Zs are at least not

as openly argumentative, and I think generally a little more open. Ten to fifteen years ago it wasn't uncommon in youth ministry to see kids turning up with LGBT pins ready for a fight. Nowadays, I don't see that quite as much.

Swimming against the tide of secular culture is a concern of each of the groups we researched. One Youth 2000 retreatant commented that she was drawn to attend thanks to the opportunity to discuss faith openly with other young people. 'This was at a time when I wasn't sure about how to live my faith in everyday society', she said. The Dominican Sisters share a story of an 11-year-old girl which epitomises the struggle and demonstrates the need for ongoing discipleship to help young people sustain a lifestyle of faith. Sr Angela Marie shared Melissa's story with her permission:

> From the time she was 11 years old, Melissa was one of the most eager youth group members. She attended every retreat possible, and always engaged on a deep emotional level in prayer on these retreats… Melissa's parents split up when she was 13, and Melissa stopped attending Mass… She drifted away from the Church but always stayed connected to youth group and appreciated Adoration. She says she didn't feel welcome at Church because of the LGBT theology, although she never experienced particular negative comments at Church. During her last year at school, Melissa attended [a Catholic youth festival] and experienced a powerful physical healing. She kept her faith internally. Melissa always valued Catholic role models from her time in youth group, and because of this accepted three invitations [in the summer of 2023] to attend a pilgrimage in the Holy Land, World Youth Day in Portugal, and [a Catholic summer camp] on the service team. From all of these, she discovered that the Catholic faith truly does bring her soul alive, and she did not want to jump back into a secular lifestyle. She decided to become a missionary for one year

in [a diocesan retreat centre] and is excited to see what sort of mission experiences God has for her in the future to help others discover the love and joy of a relationship with God.

The evidence indicates that young people need many converging supports to sustain their faith: retreats and pilgrimages as well as regular community life. Mentoring is a critical success factor too. The Barna survey recorded that 74% of committed Christian teenagers had not been mentored: they reported having no one in their life to help them grow spiritually or model prayer for them. Assigning every member of their worship academy with a mentor, One Hope Project has found mentoring to be a significant component of discipling young people. Joe and Pippa said, 'Our work has discipleship at its heart, trying not just to model worship for young people but to invest in them personally and to encourage them on their journey of faith.'

★★★

The Ascent could be described as another 'sacred umbrella' of young people, and Will Desmond, its founder, goes further in explaining why ongoing discipleship and mentoring are so fundamental.

Unsurprisingly, a typical weekend at The Ascent involves many of the elements we have already encountered in other ministries and conferences: kerygmatic proclamation, Adoration, Confession, beautiful liturgy, and worship. But what is unique to the experience of the young people at these weekends is what is called 'carousel and activation'. In three thirty minute segments over the weekend, young people connect with a mentor to reflect on what God is asking them to do as a result of the weekend. 'Activation' is a moment when young people then share what God has done and is asking of them, in a way that keeps them accountable to peers and leaders. At other weekends throughout the year, in weekly small groups and in mentoring, this is repeated. 'We believe this model of accountability is key to the growth of the young people as disciples', says Will. His claims are backed up by numerous testimonies from graduates, one of whom said that it 'provided me with the formation I needed to live unashamedly and fearlessly for God, as an adult and university student in the twenty-first century.'

What is critical to the success of The Ascent is that it is a three-year discipleship process, rather than a one-off event. The three years are an experience 'of belonging and training, to equip young people with tools to become effective missionary disciples.' Since 2013, 280 young people have been through the discipleship process, with an impressive 88% finishing the full three years. Every year, over 400 hours of mentoring is delivered by trained mentors, while 500 hours of small group sessions are delivered by a team of over fifty dedicated young adults.

Will shares how the process equips young people to swim against the tide. 'One of my favourite stories was of a teenage girl who was the only person in her Religious Studies class in a Catholic school to stand up for pro-life in an abortion debate', he says. 'She was from a faithful Catholic family but when her parents asked her why she had done it she said that it was her experience of The Ascent which had given her the confidence to make such a stand.'

Giving Back: Growth in Leadership

A generational attribute identified by Barna in their 2023 survey of Gen Z is 'drive'.[24] The survey revealed how career-driven and success-oriented Gen Z is, qualities which are certainly witnessed in the young people featured in our research. Yet, notably, focus on their careers does not consume young Catholics to the exclusion of their mission as lay disciples. Frequently, we saw young adults fostering an impressive combination of studies and professional life with voluntary engagement in the Church's mission. Interestingly, Barna notes that the 'driven' quality of Gen Z presents an opportunity for

---

[24] See <https://www.barna.com/the-open-generation/>.

the Church to engage in what could be called 'vocational discipleship... This means teaching young people about the integration of faith and occupation, helping them to better understand the concept of calling and emphasising the meaning and theological significance of work (not just their potential for professional or financial success).'

★★★

In some final glimpses into 'sacred umbrellas' of British young people, we consider the Young Christian Workers (YCW) Impact groups, and we return to look at how The Ascent develops young people into leaders.

Stephanie, a 20-year-old university student, gives up her Christmas Day back home in Greater Manchester to serve lunches to those who would otherwise have none. She says, 'It's not just the elderly who the meals are made for; families who are going through hard times are referred by social services, so we also collect good quality toys and wrap them for the children.' On Christmas Eve and Christmas Day, Stephanie together with the other members of the Young Christian Workers Impact group in her parish provide both a takeaway service and a café. 'We help with the production line preparing hot meals and desserts which are then delivered by volunteers... Many homeless, elderly people, those feeling isolated and families in need, come to the café for food, company and entertainment. It's great to be a part of this and really rewarding! It's a way of linking life and faith through action.'

Of all the groups we explored, YCW is by far the most established, having been founded in Belgium in the 1920s.[25]

---

[25] Young Christian Workers is the English translation of *Jeunesse ouvrière chrétienne* (JOC), as the movement is known in French-speaking countries. On its early development, and theological vision, see Patricia Kelly, 'Taking Theology to Work: Ressourcement Theology and Industrial Work in Interwar France and Belgium', PhD thesis, Durham University, 2016, 108–117.

In other words, it has over 65 years of existence over the other ministries featured in this chapter. YCW has evolved to meet the needs of the twenty-first century young adult, and weekly meetings focussing on 'Review of Life' enable young people to reflect on their lives and local communities from a faith perspective, to ask what change God might be inviting them to bring to their homes, workplaces, schools, and colleges. National Training and Development Officer, Anne-Marie Johnson, explains how more emphasis is now given to training young people to be Christian leaders in life through taking action. Many young people who have been involved in YCW have 'become community leaders, councillors, political activists, politicians – roles that enable them to bring about change; helping them link their faith and life through action', she says. It is certainly an approach that effectively harnesses the 'drive' of Gen Z.

Already we have seen the link between faith and social action in the interconnectedness between Generation Hope and Mary's Meals. The participants in YCW Impact are impressive witnesses to the same connection. 19-year-old student Michael speaks about how he, together with the twenty other members of his Impact group, use the 'See, Judge, Act'[26] methodology to determine a Christian response to needs in the local community. He comments, 'Often the action feels like a humanitarian response; like when our group did a sponsored sleepout to raise money for a refugee project that the parish were involved in, welcoming and housing a Syrian refugee family.'

For both Stephanie and Michael, the experiences have been pivotal for their growth as leaders. Stephanie says, 'I have developed leadership skills, preparing and leading discussions and

---

[26] See Patricia Kelly, '"See, Judge, Act": The foundation of the Citizens Project?' in Ann Marie Mealey, Pam Jarvis, Jonathan Doherty, Jan Fook (eds), *Everyday Social Justice and Citizenship: Perspectives for the 21st Century* (London: Routledge, 2017), chap. 3.

meetings, public speaking, teamwork, and planning and carrying out actions. By taking on responsibility, I have grown in confidence over the years.'

Chris, 34, also attests to the connection he has experienced through YCW between social action and personal relationship with God: '[YCW] welcomed me and helped me channel my thoughts through reflection, rooted in faith, via a very powerful process: see, judge, act. It gave me the courage to challenge wrongfulness, to speak up, and to lead. It also helped me reconnect with my faith and open up a personal relationship with God, through Jesus's teachings.' The growth in confidence and leadership signalled by these young people seem to mirror the similar growth in Gateacre and Richmond parishioners witnessing to their faith cited in the previous chapter.

★★★

Like Chris, young adults in The Ascent reflect on their gratitude for all that they received through the process: a gratitude that is poured back in a spirit of generosity to younger generations. An impressive group of graduates in their twenties shares how the Ascent prepared them for leadership and service. Joe says of himself and his friends: 'we are very willing to make, sometimes considerable, sacrifices in our free time to [serve younger people in the Ascent process]. The impact of on each of us here certainly cannot be understated.'

The Ascent's use of mentoring has been abundantly fruitful for this group of young Catholics: the cumulative impact of over ten years of this discipleship process has paid dividends for the wider Church.

Marcus, a young adult who now leads Joel's Bar, another Catholic youth conference, attributes the formation he received from The Ascent as providing 'a bedrock of Catholic teaching, personal encounter through the Holy Spirit and spiritual accompaniment that took me from a place of being nominally Catholic to striving for Christ to be at the heart of all I do every day.' Anna agrees. Currently studying for a Master's in bioethics and working as a fundraiser for another Catholic charity, it was The Ascent, she says, that 'gave me incredible foundations in leadership and discipleship, in being bold in faith, and to always trust in the Lord and follow his call.' She now leads a small group for other young people.

Eric is a manager on the largest submarine cable project ever. He says that The Ascent 'equipped me to think about my life and what it could be, bringing God into my day-to-day decision making and acknowledging that I have been created to be full in spirit as well as attain fullness in all other areas of life.' It equipped him to live out his faith in a previous role in international infrastructure at a Big Tech company. As well as forming him for professional life, it was The Ascent that inspired Eric to work with three other students to found Catholic Student Network. Of The Ascent he says, 'I am continually impressed by how it builds up young people in faith and is the leading light for post-Confirmation formation that exists in the current Church that I am aware of.'

What is consistent across each ministry's account is how a deepening of relationship with God flows into leadership and service: action is not decoupled from growth in faith. A testimony from a 30-year-old participant in One Hope Project encapsulates this well:

> [In the training] I was brought deep into the core of why we worship and learned how to lead myself into worship before leading others. The session on liturgy was a profound one for me in particular. It had led me to reflect on how I behaved previously when serving in the music group. If Mass music is a 'soundtrack' of what is going on at the altar, I realised I was

focussing too much on my music sheets and my instrument instead of having my eyes on the altar. It was such a freeing realisation and once my focus had shifted, I found lots of joy in the service, the work became easy. 'Eyes on the altar, always' has now become my new mantra in everything I do. I will carry this and share with anyone who is discerning about answering the Lord's call.

Family, School, Parish?

The traditional triadic strategy of family-school-parish for faith transmission has a somewhat revered status and is still referred to today.[27] Yet the evidence suggests that this model was not working well even thirty, forty, or fifty years ago,[28] let alone in our considerably more secular milieu today. On the question of schools, Bullivant and Clements report that,

> [O]ur findings suggest that attending Catholic schools has little to no *independent* influence over adult religiosity. This might seem surprising, given the considerable resources the Church devotes to supporting its network of around 2600 primary and secondary schools across Britain. Furthermore, one might prima facie assume that the cumulative hours of Catholic-inflected religious education, Masses, prayer, sacramental preparation, and indeed interaction and friendship with other Catholic peers would amount to a notable boost to religious socialisation, over and above what is (or is not) received within the family environment. However, this seems not to be the case.

---

[27] Here is just one diocesan example: <https://www.dioceseofsalford.org.uk/wp-content/uploads/Fostering-good-relations-between-Home-School-Parish.pdf>.

[28] Stephen Bullivant, *Mass Exodus: Catholic Disaffiliation in Britain and America since Vatican II* (Oxford: Oxford University Press, 2019), 189–222.

Recognising Hornsby-Smith's assessment in 1987 that attendance at a Catholic school contributed only in a 'very small' way to subsequent adult practice, they surmise that such an effect has, today, 'dried up completely'.[29]

The disintegration of the 'sacred canopy' is precisely a disintegration of institutional means of faith transmission, and why the parishes featured in chapter one are altering their approach so radically. As families weaken across society as a whole and as the number of Catholic marriages plummets,[30] families are not the critical factor, as they might once have been, in ongoing practice into adulthood. In fact, being brought up Catholic today is a good predictor of *not* identifying as Catholic as an adult. According to Bullivant and Clements,

> One recent estimate, drawing on pooled BSA data, showed that 48% of those born between 1985 and 1998 (i.e., equating to the 18–24 and 25–34 cohorts in the current data) were now 'nones,' compared to 36% of those born between 1945 and 1964—which was itself a significant rise on the preceding decades' cradle Catholics.

Indeed, in our data, parish or school are mentioned only in relation to the para-institutional ministry (i.e., outside of the normal diocesan parish and school structures) that is effective where the primary institution is not: the schools that take their students to the Generation Hope camp; the parish where the Dominican Sisters

---

[29] Ben Clements and Stephen Bullivant, 'Why Younger Catholics Seem More Committed: Survivorship Bias and/or "Creative Minority" Effects among British Catholics', *Journal for the Scientific Study of Religion*, 61.2 (2022), 450–75, at 469.

[30] There were 52,601 Catholic marriages in Britain in 1971; 29,250 in 1990; 9,328 in 2019. See Timothy Kinnear, 'Statistical Appendices', in Alana Harris (ed.), *The Oxford History of British and Irish Catholicism, Vol. 5: Recapturing the Apostolate of the Laity, 1914–2021* (Oxford: Oxford University Press, 2023), 357–76, at 370.

run a youth group.[31] It is not possible to make the same claims about families, of course, but what we do know is that faith is more likely handed on in families where Catholic belief and identity are 'backed up' with intentional practice.

Conclusion

It is likely that, of the young Catholics aged 18 to 34 who attend Mass weekly, when spread across the sprawling network of 2533 British parishes, only a small handful are seated in your parish's pews any given Sunday. The pain and bewilderment expressed by older generations in the national synthesis report for the Synod is therefore understandable: young people do not have visibility in parishes even if their commitment is higher than older generations. But when we start to look at the Catholic Church in Britain not through the institutional system of parishes covering every geographic territory but rather non-institutionally – in terms of networks and communities of disciples – a different picture emerges. Gen Z Catholics, owing to their small numbers, have a different, non-institutional pattern of engagement with the Church which differs from previous generations but is nonetheless real and vibrant.

The movements, ministries and conferences featured in this chapter represent only a slice of a larger picture: many others do extraordinary work with young people that are not named in these

---

[31] There are, thankfully, some instances where, owing to far-sighted individuals within the institutional setting, an institution can learn from the critical success factors of fruitful Catholic youth ministries. One Catholic retreat centre director commented that, in the past, the retreat centre tended to be seen as 'a "come here for a nice few days" sort of operation… Most were conceived in the 1960s and 1970s when Catholic schools had a lot of practising Catholics.' Students were brought on retreat for 'a bit of a pastoral boost.' Today there is a 'new dynamic in which the average subset of kids in a Catholic secondary school will be little different to your average group of kids. This needs a different approach, one which recognises that the work is actually often "first principles" evangelisation/ kerygma.' In other words, fruit for young people comes when the programme embraces Catholic distinctiveness, fostering a creative minority. Having consciously made this shift at the retreat centre he leads, he says 'we are starting to see the first signs of real evangelisation.'

pages. A second major locus of young adult Catholicity – university chaplaincies and CathSocs – is the subject of a separate chapter (four). Yet even the few we have explored engage with thousands of young people every year, including many 'nones'. The young people we have spotlighted in this chapter are at the heart of these movements and ministries, and their passion and commitment – if not their numbers – should give us cause for hope.

What conclusions might we draw from the witnesses of these young people?

First, that their experience of belonging is strongly tied to, and sustained by, the para-institutional initiatives we have featured. This is something we will see in other chapters too.

Second, the movements and initiatives we featured are not, on the whole, local communities but rather national ones. This may be counter-intuitive when we consider our assumptions of what having or belonging to a 'sacred umbrella' entails, but the events, online meetings, and regular accompaniment over the course of a year serve to unite young people in national networks. In The Ascent's publicity we read, 'Be connected to a national group of young Catholics who are on the same journey.' When grouped nationally, they are more visible. While older generations might not experience the presence of the young adults featured in this chapter, it is striking that younger teenagers (e.g. at the Generation Hope camp, and through Ascent mentoring) do. This appears to be a further critical factor for fruitfulness which is possible only on a national scale: young adults in their twenties ministering to teenagers.

Third, many of the groups featured show how multiple, converging experiences are needed to initiate and nurture young people into an ongoing relationship with God. A picture was formed of a holistic mosaic, building faith from many different angles and perspectives, and serving the whole person. Conferences, pilgrimages, and festivals need to be combined with small groups, friendships, and mentoring. Prayerful opportunities for sacramental encounters are combined with games or outdoor activity. Certain elements were referenced repeatedly: Adoration, Confession, beautiful liturgy, and contemporary praise and worship music.

Fourth and finally, it is important to consider the cumulative impact of ten plus years of the work of many of these groups and ministries. The number of vocations attributed to Youth 2000 thanks to thirty years of its existence is impressive, and, given the depth of faith and formation of young adults emerging from The Ascent today, it remains to be seen how dramatically they too will continue to bear fruit for the Church's flourishing. Seedling ministries such as these, because para-institutional, receive little or no central Church funding. When we consider the fruits of a tiny Catholic ministry with, in some cases, a single full-time employee, is it not time to divert funds and resources towards non-institutional ministries punching well above their weight? More generous resourcing of these ministries from the institutional Church could radically re-route the current trajectory. Undeniably, very courageous decisions (perhaps unthinkable to previous generations) would need to be taken, but these small ministries indicate that the future story could be very different. Indeed, thousands more young people could be filling the pews of Catholic parishes on a Sunday morning.

3. Diasporas

'Rock concert mosh pit' is perhaps not the most reached-for analogy when describing British church services. Nevertheless, it was an apt appraisal of the density – though not at all of the dress or demeanour – of worshippers thronging the Cathedral's oval nave. Even marked into 'zones' with duct tape, and carefully policed by a team of volunteer marshals, it was rammed. Up in the balcony, though also full, things were more spaced out thanks to the rows of seats. Even so, we also stood for much of the liturgy. Judging from the steady flow of people, carrying wicker baskets of bread covered in ornately decorated cloths, going up from or down to the basement, a substantial number were in there at any one time too. (According to the helpfully bilingual Bulletin, this blessing of food had been going on the whole afternoon and evening. Confession was available even longer: 9 am to 10 pm.) All in all, I[1] estimated attendance at around 800. It's difficult to assize the relative proportions of socio-demographic groups in so large and packed a congregation. There seemed to be good numbers of men, women, and children; a full spectrum of ages, with perhaps particular spikes among the over-60s and those in their 20s and 30s; and the full gamut of bags from 'designer hand' to 'supermarket carrier'. A significant proportion of the congregation were clearly at home, knowing where to go and what to do, and greeting fellow parishioners. Plenty of others, though perfectly comfortable with the service – when to stand, when to cross oneself, when and what

[1] SB.

to sing – seemed less familiar with the building itself; occasional visitors, making a special effort to be here today, instead of their usual places of worship. I also spied one or two younger men turn up, stay only long enough to honestly say they'd been, and take a quick selfie on their way out. No doubt their far-off mothers were pleased to receive them.

This was only the first of two such liturgies that evening. The next day, Easter Sunday in the Julian calendar, there would be a further six. Assuming similar attendance at each, that's a good six thousand or so worshippers. The venue? Central London's *other* Catholic Cathedral: the beautiful Ukrainian one, dedicated to the Holy Family. Tucked away just off Oxford St, this former congregationalist chapel was acquired by the Ukrainian exarchate in 1967. The exarchate had been established ten years prior, responsible for the pastoral care of c. 25,000 Ukrainian Catholics living in Britain after World War II.[2] It was elevated to a full eparchy, the Eastern Catholic equivalent of a diocese, in 2013, underlining the significance and permanence of the Ukrainian Catholic presence here. Of the twenty-three Eastern Catholic churches – many of which have an active presence in Britain, as we shall see – only the Ukrainian and Syro-Malabar Churches have so far attained full eparchial status.

The above visit occurred in 2019. This was, therefore, before the Russian invasion of Ukraine in February 2022. This initially meant a decline in numbers, as many men returned to fight. This was swiftly followed by an influx of refugees, under the

---

[2] See Athanasius McVay, "For this Family in Exile": The Ukrainian Greek-Catholic Church in Great Britain, a History Part 1 (1890–1970)', draft manuscript; Roman Krawec, 'Ukrainian Catholic Church in Great Britain' (2022), Ukrainians in the United Kingdom: Online Encyclopedia, *https://www.ukrainiansintheuk.info/eng/03/ucc-e.htm*. Strictly speaking, the Exarchate was originally founded for England and Wales in 1957. Scotland was added in 1968. We are grateful to Fr McVay and Fr Mark Woodruff, Cathedral clergy past and present, for additional information about the Ukrainian Catholic community in Britain.

government's Ukraine Family Scheme and Ukraine Sponsorship Schemes. The Home Office's statistics give c. 190,000 new arrivals between March 2022 and September 2023. How many of these are Catholic is hard to know, but if it is roughly equal to the one-in-ten in Ukraine as a whole, then that's 19,000. This has naturally meant that the Cathedral, which was already a major focal point for the Ukrainian Catholic diaspora (hence the numbers travelling in for Easter, whether from elsewhere in London or further afield), has acquired even greater importance. This is partly symbolic, as a powerful witness to a free Ukraine in the heart of London, and as the venue for major events, with recent visitors including the King, Ukraine's First Lady, and current and former UK prime ministers. But it is also deeply practical. Alongside its more obvious religious functions, the Cathedral community has always been a major provider of formal and informal support for Ukrainians in the capital. The horrors of the Russian War have dramatically increased these needs, both for the British Ukrainians already here, and especially for the large numbers of recent arrivals, many of whom arrive with little or no English, and into less-than-ideal living situations.[3] Within months of the invasion, the Cathedral opened a Ukrainian Welcome Centre in its basement, in partnership with the Association of Ukrainians in Great Britain, to act both as a 'single point of contact for all essential information for arrival, settling and long-term living in the UK', and to provide in-person help including English classes, art therapy, and mother-and-baby groups.[4] These are, needless to say, open to all Ukrainians, whether Catholic or not.

---

[3] See James Jeffrey, 'Ukrainian Catholic Community in UK Count the Costs and Kindnesses at Two-year Anniversary of Russian Invasion', *Catholic Herald*, 22 February 2024 <https://catholicherald.co.uk/uks-ukrainian-catholic-community-count-the-costs-and-kindnesses-at-two-year-anniversary-of-russian-invasion/>.

[4] See <https://www.ukrainianwelcomecentre.org/>.

Upstairs, attendance is unsurprisingly up, swelled both by refugees and the formerly lapsed.[5] Easter 2023, for example, required even more services than did 2019. But even a regular Sunday now sees 2,500-3,000 worshippers at the Cathedral. If that sounds like a lot, it's because it is. (For comparison, the Anglican Westminster Abbey gets 950 on a typical Sunday.[6]) Indeed, if the Cathedral of the Holy Family were Protestant rather than Eastern Catholic, it would easily fulfil the standard numerical criterion for 'megachurch' status.[7] There are also good numbers at the growing number of satellite 'mission points' in and around London. Some of these had been planned even before February 2022, including a regular English language Divine Liturgy aimed principally at younger, second- and third-generation British Ukrainians. The War has of course made the case more urgent (and indeed persuasive to the Latin-rite parishes hosting them). It helps that the clergy are well-practised at pastoral entrepreneurship in the face of adversity. In early 2021,

---

[5] Steve Bruce's theory of 'cultural defence' as a counter-secularizing force is perhaps a useful one here: where there are two (or more) communities in conflict and they are of different religions (for example, Protestants and Catholics in Ulster, or Serbs, Croats and Bosnian Muslims in what used to be Yugoslavia), then the religious identity of each can acquire a new significance and call forth a new loyalty as religious identity becomes a way of expressing ethnic pride and laying claim to what Max Weber called 'ethnic honour': the sense of 'the excellence of one's own customs and the inferiority of alien ones'. Similarly when there is a people with a common religion dominated by an external force (of either a different religion or none at all), then religious institutions acquire an additional purpose as defenders of the culture and identity of the people. (*Religion in the Modern World: From Cathedrals to Cults* [Oxford: Oxford University Press, 1996], 96; see also his *God is Dead: Secularization in the West* [Oxford: Oxford University Press, 2002], 31–4). It is likely that Ukrainian Orthodoxy – i.e., versus *Russian* Orthodoxy – functions in a similar way for its adherents too.

[6] Church of England, *Cathedral Statistics 2022* (Church House, 2024), 24, available online: <https://www.churchofengland.org/sites/default/files/2024-02/cathedral-statistics-2022.pdf>.

[7] E.g., 'The term megachurch generally refers to any Protestant… Christian congregation with a sustained average weekly attendance of 2000 persons or more in its worship services, counting all adults and children at all its worship locations' ('Megachurch definition', Hartford Institute for Religion Research, <http://hirr.hartsem.edu/megachurch/definition.html>). A good number of other Catholic churches in Britain would comfortably meet that attendance criterion.

with considerable Covid-related distancing regulations in place, the Cathedral itself offered up to *eighteen* services every Sunday; two every two hours, with parallel services in the main church and basement. Even so, demand far outstripped supply.

While the situation in London is exceptional, Ukrainian parishes (some now with satellites of their own) exist throughout England – in the East and West Midlands, and with a particular cluster in the North West – as well as in Edinburgh. However, the existing infrastructure was situated to meet earlier generations' pastoral requirements. Where jobs were fifty or sixty years ago is not necessarily where they are today, and more recent, pre-2022, Ukrainian immigrants often gravitated elsewhere in the country. Thus not all churches are in a sufficient state of repair to be useful in the present hour of need.[8] As such, while many Ukrainian Catholic parishes are now (re)thriving – our July 2022 visit to Leicester's Ascension of Our Lord church found a good mix of East European and East Midlands accents, for example – there is likely a good deal of unmet demand elsewhere in the country. Since it is probable that a significant proportion of refugees will choose to remain in Britain indefinitely, then it is to be hoped that creative ways are found to meet, resource, and nurture this population into the future.

Diasporic communities

As noted in the Introduction, immigration is a major contributor to most every area of British Catholic life. The British Ukrainian community is a particularly striking example, and one with a good deal of current salience. But dozens of country-specific stories could, and somewhere should, be told.

---

[8] For example, thanks to an out-of-date website, a summer 2021 visit to the Ukrainian church in Bolton was met with locked gates, overgrown grass, and a distinctly derelict vibe. The Bolton community, now boosted by refugees, has since found a regular Sunday home in a local Latin parish.

However, it is not immigration per se that is the subject of this chapter. Rather, our focus here is on specific sorts of liturgical communities, catering primarily to those from a particular national and/or linguistic background. These come in two main types. The first are Latin-rite Catholics, who regularly attend Mass (and/or other liturgical or devotional events) in a language other than English. The second are Eastern Catholics, attending a Divine Liturgy, Qurbana/o, or some differently named 'Mass-equivalent'. This will also *probably* be in a language other than English (either a liturgical language, or a foreign vernacular, or a mix), though not necessarily.[9] In practice, these two types often share a great deal in common, not least in typically drawing their congregations from a much wider geographical area than does a typical diocesan parish (something they also share with Latin Mass congregations, see chapter five, and several of the super-parishes attracting worshippers from well beyond their formal boundaries, see chapter one). However, as explored below, there are special reasons why Eastern Catholic communities should be treated separately.

According to data from the 2019 'Catholics in Britain' survey, 9% of British weekly Mass-goers say that they most often attend Mass in a modern language other than English.[10] Even if that figure might be a little on the high side,[11] it still represents a notable segment of active Catholics. These Masses happen in various ways. At the most solidly established end of

---

[9] The Ukrainian eparchy's introduction of English-language Divine Liturgies was noted above. The Syro-Malabar also offers the Qurbana in English, not least for its growing numbers of British-born children.

[10] Stephen Bullivant, 'Mass Markets and the "Liturgical Long Tail"', *Antiphon*, 1–25, at 17.

[11] There is some evidence from other responses to the question that some respondents used their answers to express their *preferred* type of Mass – i.e., the one they would attend most frequently, if able – rather than what they actually most frequently attend. If so, then this would be an interesting special case of the phenomenon of 'over-reporting', where churchgoers appear to 'round up' their level of attendance to the one they wish (others to think) they actually manage.

things, there are a relatively small number of dedicated parishes or 'mission churches' for specific national/linguistic groups. By far the largest, and most geographically spread, group of these are the Polish parishes, in the care of the Polish Catholic Missions of England and Wales (est. 1894, though substantially expanded after World War Two) and Scotland (est. 1948). South of the border, the Mission has twenty-nine churches and thirteen chapels of its own, with the clergy – sent directly by the Polish bishops to serve the diaspora – assigned to them often also offering Polish Masses at other local parishes.[12] North of the border, Polish parishes more commonly cohabit with ordinary diocesan parishes, often with a Polish priest running both. In practice, this frequently results – as at Sacred Heart/*Serca Jezusa*, Aberdeen, or St Anne's/*Świętej Anny*, Glasgow – in a single, bilingual parish.[13] Like the Ukrainian churches, many of these parishes were set up in the immediate post-war decades, and their fortunes have waned and (more recently) waxed depending on migration. Unlike the Ukrainians, however, Brexit will surely affect numbers in the longer term. Yet for the time being, pastoral business appears to be booming. The English and Welsh mission acquired two new churches, in Swindon and Corby, as recently as 2018.

On a more modest scale, a handful of groups have a permanent church base in London: St Casimir, Bethnal Green, for

---

[12] On England and Wales, see Polish Catholic Mission, *The Polish Catholic Mission in England and Wales* (London: Polish Catholic Mission, 2005); Kerry Gallagher and Marta Trzebiatowska, 'Becoming a "Real" Catholic: Polish Migrants and Lived Religiosity in the UK and Ireland', *Journal of Contemporary Religion* 32/3, 431–45; Marek Wódka, Stanisław Fel, and Jarosław Kozak, 'Religiosity of Polish Catholics in the UK: Attitude towards Faith, Affiliation, Membership and Religious Practices', *Religions* 11/8 (2020), 1–13.

[13] On Scotland, see Michał Adam Palacz, 'Polish Diasporic Catholicism in Scotland', in Rubina Ramji and Alison Marshall (eds), *The Bloomsbury Handbook of Religion and Migration* (London: Bloomsbury, 2022), 55–72; Marta Trzebiatowska, 'The Advent of the "EasyJet Priest": Dilemmas of Polish Catholic Integration in the UK', *Sociology*, 44/6, 1055–72. For the mentioned parish websites, see <https://www.sacredhearttorry.com/> and <https://www.swanna.uk/?fbclid=IwAR3PAClB7Pmtzme81GWbygNI9zb4c5DgB9e6aFbj399QeW4A98eKSL4pDVM>.

Lithuanians;[14] Notre Dame de France, Soho, for the highly diverse global Francophone community; St Boniface, Whitechapel, for German speakers; St Peter's, Holborn, for Italians. Here and in other big cities, many other groups will have a designated 'chaplain', who is usually a priest on staff at a regular parish. This church then serves as a co-ordinating hub for those in the wider area, organising Masses, events, etc., alongside the usual English-language pastoral programme. Some archdioceses – Westminster, Southwark, Birmingham – have dozens of such 'ethnic chaplains'.[15] For the largest language groups, this might amount to multiple weekly Masses, regular Confession times, prayer groups and Bible studies, special events for cherished saints' days, and so on. For others, Masses might be monthly – 'second Sundays at 2pm', say– or more irregular still. Every chaplaincy is different, and much depends both on the local density of a given group and, naturally, the availability of willing and able clergy. Sometimes, the full size of a large-but-dispersed community is only apparent (at least to outsiders) when they come together for a regional or national event. To give just one example, while Tamil-language Masses are thin on the ground,[16] the annual Tamil Walsingham pilgrimage is the country's largest. In recent years, this has drawn 15-20,000 in a single day (albeit including a significant minority of Sri Lankan

---

[14] Emily Gilbert, 'The Lithuanian Catholic Church and the Lithuanian Community in Great Britain', *Changing Identities: Latvians, Lithuanians and Estonians in Britain*, 2 December 2015, https://changingidentities.wordpress.com/2015/12/02/the-lithuanian-catholic-church-and-the-lithuanian-community-in-great-britain/.

[15] Breda Gray and Louise Ryan, 'Migration, Migrant Chaplaincy, and Multi-Ethnic Britain', in Alana Harris (ed.), *The Oxford History of British and Irish Catholicism, Vol. 5: Recapturing the Apostolate of the Laity, 1914–2021* (Oxford: Oxford University Press, 2023), 291–307.

[16] As of March 2024, the Tamil Chaplaincy advertises monthly Sunday Masses at a dozen different churches, all in the southern half of England (with Coventry and Milton Keynes being the most northerly). Only in London could one hope to attend a Tamil Mass every week, and only then by going to different churches at different times each Sunday afternoon. See: https://www.tamil-rcchaplaincy.org.uk/chaplaincy/year-planner/.

Hindus).[17] Numbers are so large, and congestion on local roads so great, that the Shrine's calendar now features 'Tamil One' (May) and 'Tamil Two' (July) to spread the strain.

Finally, a significant amount of provision comes about fairly informally, depending largely on which priests happen to be where at any one time, and/or on which communities have a sufficiently large or organised laity in any one place to *get* a priest in from somewhere else (if only for the afternoon). It is natural for foreign priests on loan to British dioceses to connect with diaspora communities, and find ways to serve them 'on the side', while here. To give a single example, Nigeria's Missionary Society of St Paul (MSP) has several dozen priests serving in English, Welsh, and Scottish parishes. Given how large the West African Catholic diaspora here is, they need not travel far to find ways to help out. British priests who have studied or ministered abroad, or are themselves from particular diaspora communities, might also put their language skills and cultural knowledge to good use. It is also not unheard of for a parish priest to learn a new language in order better to serve his flock. For example, we know of one priest in Salford Diocese who took up Polish, and now can preach and say Mass in it. There are no doubt other such examples, perhaps many.

Much of this provision is necessarily quite precarious: depending on which priests, with which skills, happen to be where. Many priests engaged, formally or informally, in this kind of ministry travel large distances to offer Mass, often on top of their own parish responsibilities. Should that priest return home, be

---

[17] Richard Antony, 'British-born Tamils: A Study of Young Tamil Londoners' (2012), unpublished PhD thesis, University of Surrey, UK. We are grateful to Dr Antony for providing additional, up-to-date information on the Tamil diaspora. On shared Tamil Hindu/Catholic devotions in a London parish, see also Alana Harris, '"They Just Dig St Antony, He's Right Up Their Street, Religious Wise": Transnational Flows and Inter-Religious Encounters in an East London Parish', in Dominic Pasura and Marta Bivand Erdal (eds), *Migration, Transnationalism and Catholicism* (London: Palgrave Macmillan, 2016), 95–120.

reassigned, retire, or indeed 'burn out', then what may have been a weekly or monthly Mass with a stable community can suddenly be in doubt. Church space too is often only temporary, relying on parishes with a suitable window in their own weekend schedules (hence the odd times such Masses tend to be at). For both reasons, while setting up a new regular Mass in a given place is hard enough, keeping one going over years or even decades is harder still. And that's without taking into account such things as altar servers, music, refreshments (which, especially on feast days, might include celebratory meals), advertising, and tidying up. Where such diasporic gathered communities – to coin a cumbersome phrase – exist, one necessarily also finds a core group of highly committed laity organising everything.

The role that these diasporic communities, including the Eastern Catholic ones, play in the wider Catholic ecosystem is significantly underappreciated. This is, in part, because they tend to be hidden from most Mass-goers. That is no one's fault. After all, why should a non-speaker think to turn up at a Mass in Konkani, Tagalog, Korean, or Portuguese, even *if* they are aware that there is a regular service in their own church? (And to be fair, they may well not be, since these 'off-menu items' are not always advertised in the regular parish bulletin.) Even parish priests who generously host one or more such groups in their own church may be unaware of the existence or extent of other groups in other churches in the area.

But if one makes a point of going to such services every so often, one soon realises just how much there is going on. Turn up one Sunday afternoon at a pebbledash church in Lanarkshire for an advertised liturgy in Malayalam, and find over 500 first and second-generation Keralans midway through seven hours of prayer, catechesis, bible study, Adoration, dance lessons, and more. Walk past a suburban church in Oxfordshire on a Saturday afternoon and, noticing the coloured banners unfurled outside, on a whim join hundreds of Filipinos, waving handkerchiefs, singing Tagalog worship songs, and plying curious interlopers' children with snacks. These Filipinos are members of the millions-strong charismatic movement El Shaddai, whose rallies regularly draw hundreds of thousands in Manila.[18] Visit the same church at noon a few days before Christmas and find the weekly Polish Mass there full, standing-room only, with boxes of free *opłatki* (traditional wafers, richly decorated with Nativity scenes) to take home so that one can celebrate *Wigilia* properly.

While these anecdotes – all true, taken from our fieldwork – barely scratch the surface, they should at least hint at the considerable 'religious capital' present in these diasporic liturgical/devotional communities. At one level, this is not surprising. In the first place, high levels of secularity in Britain mean that immigrants from most countries hail from contexts with much higher norms of religious belief, practice, and belonging. Furthermore, one has to be highly invested to attend these Masses, often a long way from where one actually lives (costing both time and money), and at odd times on a Saturday or Sunday afternoon. This is all the truer for those trekking to full-day regional or national events, such as the two mentioned above or AFCM's 'Second Saturdays' conventions discussed in the Introduction. However one divides up British Mass-goers, and bearing in mind that attending church weekly is itself now the preserve of a comparative hard core of baptised Catholics, these must count as among the hardest of the hard core.

Such commitment must not, however, be taken for granted. Being highly religious is not something 'essential' to being Polish, Ukrainian, Keralan, Sri Lankan, Filipino, Vietnamese, or Ghanaian. (After all, people used to say the same thing about being Irish.) It is true that some migrants maintain their existing religiosity on

---

[18] Katharine L. Wiegele, *Investing in Miracles: El Shaddai and the Transformation of Popular Catholicism in the Philippines* (Honolulu: University of Hawaii Press, 2005); Esmeralda Fortunato-Sanchez and Thomas M. Landy, 'El Shaddai and the Charismatic Transformation of Philippine Catholicism', <https://www.catholicsandcultures.org/philippines-el-shaddai-serves-largest-population-charismatic-followers>.

coming to Britain. Others increase it, especially where religious contexts serve important ancillary roles. These may include providing work or accommodation contacts, offering material support (the Ukrainian Welcome Centre is an obvious example here; note too that, as well as free *opłatki*, the above Polish Mass had a table of donated clothes), or simply a space where one can find the comforting sounds, smells, and tastes of home. Sometimes you want to go where everyone can pronounce your name. Similarly, referring to the Zimbabwean Catholic congregation in Birmingham, Dominic Pasura observes:

> [It] can be described as the centre of a religious and cultural creation, a kind of a modern-day transnational extended family. It provides members with a sense of community solidarity, resources, and spiritual comfort. More importantly, it serves as some form of insurance against social exclusion, deportation, and eventualities such as death. What differentiates the transnational extended family from other social networks or migrant institutions is not only the spiritual well-being it gives to its members, but also the way in which it embeds its members in Britain, giving them a greater sense of security and belonging.[19]

If immigrants end up settling down to raise children, moreover, a significant amount of cultural activity – language lessons, traditional dance classes – often occurs in or around a religious setting.[20]

---

[19] Dominic Pasura, 'Religious Transnationalism: The case of Zimbabwean Catholics in Britain', *Journal of Religion in Africa* 42/1 (2012), 26–53, at 35–6.

[20] None of these factors are exclusive to British or Catholic contexts. On the role of Thai Buddhist temples in California as 'cultural carriers', for instance, see Todd LeRoy Perreira, '*Sasana Sakon* and the New Asian American: Intermarriage and Identity at a Thai Buddhist Temple in Silicon Valley', in Tony Carnes and Fenggang Yang (eds), *Asian American Religions: The Making and Remaking of Borders and Boundaries* (New York: New York University Press, 2004), 313–37.

However, the fact remains that large numbers of immigrants do *not* keep up the religious habits of home. As we noted in the Introduction, church attendance in Britain would be much, much higher if they did. Hence as Gallagher and Trzebiatowska observe, commenting on Poles specifically but with a good deal of wider applicability: 'The freedom associated with entering a new society provides migrants with the opportunity to reconsider their religious practices and personal faith. As a result, some turn away from the church.'[21] Also worth noting here, of course, is that the demographics of economic migrants – i.e., disproportionate numbers of young adults – mean that, both here and back home, they are likely to be less religious than the national average to begin with. Typical working patterns – long shifts, weekend hours – may not, moreover, be conducive to regular Mass-going.

High levels of religious devotion are not, therefore, automatic among diaspora populations. Nevertheless, they are, and always have been, significant net contributors to British Catholic vitality. Our diasporic congregations are by no means the only places where this can be witnessed. Most parishes will give some evidence for it, and those that are thriving often do so with abundance.[22] Even so, the

---

[21] Gallagher and Trzebiatowska, 'On Becoming a "Real" Catholic', 438. See also Wódka et al., 'Religiosity of Polish Catholics in the UK'.

[22] Some take this to an extreme. Take Holy Rood, Swindon, for example: a small flint church, to which an enormous barn-like annexe has needed to be added. It has some claim to being the best attended 'ordinary' parish church in the country. (That is, if one takes several of London's Polish churches as being, in the nicest possible way, abnormal. Westminster Cathedral parish may also get a higher Sunday attendance, though we were not able to get recent figures; it, too, can hardly be taken as a normal parish). This is thanks principally to the very large Goan diaspora in the area. On our December 2019 visit to one of the parish's five Sunday Masses, there were perhaps 600 people there, 85–90% of whom were non-White. See, e.g., Joanna P. Coelho, 'Citizenship and Nationality: The Dynamic "Home" of Goan Catholics in Swindon, England', in Ajaya K. Sahoo (ed.), *Mapping Indian Diaspora: Contestations and Representations* (New Delhi: Rawat Publications, 2017), 31–52.

More generally and diversely, for research on the significant 'immigrant boost' to at least some Catholic churches, see: Alana Harris, 'Devout East Enders: Catholicism in the East End of London', in David Goodhew (ed.), *Church Growth in London: 1980 to the Present* (Farnham: Ashgate, 2012), 41–58; Marion Bowman, Simon Coleman,

dedicated ethnic/linguistic/national communities, which largely operate on the peripheries of 'ordinary parish life', serve a particularly important function. And critically, this is true not only for the congregation members themselves, but for British Catholicism as a whole. Quite why this is so is explored in chapter five, as part of a bigger argument concerning 'niche' congregations. First, however, we need to consider the special case of Britain's Eastern Catholics.

Light from the East

Viewed in a certain way, the Catholic Church is in fact a communion made up of twenty-four distinct 'sub' Churches.[23] The Latin (Western) Church, headquartered in Rome, is by far the biggest of these, and the primacy of the Bishop of Rome – i.e., the Pope – over the whole is acknowledged by the other twenty-three 'particular Churches'. These latter, collectively described as the Eastern Catholic Churches, have their own liturgical rites, traditions, saints, and (often heroic) histories. Though it is natural to think of them as a single group, especially when distinguishing them from the Latin Church, they vary very greatly among themselves. Most, though not all, represent offshoots of the Eastern Orthodox Churches, Oriental Orthodox Churches, or the Church of the East 'returning' to full communion with Rome. Some are tiny and precarious. Others are millions-strong, transnational bodies.[24]

John Jenkins, and Tiina Sepp, 'Visibly Different: Continuity and Change at Westminster Cathedral', in David Goodhew and Anthony-Paul Cooper (eds), *The Desecularisation of the City: London's Churches, 1980 to the Present* (Abingdon: Routledge, 2019), 300–27.

[23] Cf. 'The Holy Catholic Church, which is the Mystical Body of Christ, is made up of the faithful who are organically united in the Holy Spirit by the same faith, the same sacraments and the same government and who, combining together into various groups which are held together by a hierarchy, form separate Churches or Rites' (Vatican II, *Orientalium Ecclesiarum*, 2).

[24] Useful primers can be found in Robin Gibbons, *The Eastern Churches: Understanding the Eastern Christian Churches* (London: Catholic Truth Society, 2006), 44–61; Fred J. Saato, *American Eastern Catholics* (Mahwah, NJ: Paulist Press, 2006).

DIASPORAS

So far in these pages, we have met Britain's – and the world's – two largest groups of Eastern Catholics. The Ukrainian Greek Catholic Church, which is one of three modern-day successors to a Ruthenian Uniate Church that (re)joined the Catholic Church in 1596,[25] has featured heavily in this chapter. The Syro-Malabar Catholic Church has appeared twice – in the Introduction's rainy day in West Bromwich, and in the above vignette from small-town Lanarkshire. Its roots, however, are in southwestern India, where it is among several Christian bodies (also including the Syro-Malankara Catholic Church) which credit their foundation to St Thomas the Apostle.[26] It formally united with the Catholic Church in 1599, from the Church of the East, whose East Syriac liturgical tradition it still represents. In its native Kerala, Christians constitute c.18% of the population; Syro-Malabar Catholics, the largest single group, make up around two-fifths of these.[27] The Church has eparchies (i.e., dioceses) covering much of India, as well as four outside it: Melbourne, Chicago, Mississauga (near Toronto), and Great Britain.[28]

While the Ukrainian Cathedral may be minutes from Selfridge's and the Disney Store, the Syro-Malabars' Cathedral of St Alphonsa can boast a razzamatazzier locale. It's just off the Preston ring

---

[25] Thanks to the tortuous nature of Eastern European political – and thus religious – history over the past several centuries, things are actually much more complicated than this. In its contemporary form and name, the Ukrainian Greek Catholic Church emerged in the Soviet era as an underground church in its homeland (in the face of an official programme of forced Orthodoxisation), with significant communities in exile abroad. The other two current successors to the Ruthenian Uniate Church are the Belarussian Greek Catholic Church and the Russian Greek Catholic Church. Confusingly, the present-day Ruthenian Catholic Church has a separate history.

[26] See Philip Jenkins, *The Lost History of Christianity: The Thousand-Year Golden Age of the Church in the Middle East, Africa, and Asia—and How It Died* (San Francisco, CA: HarperOne, 2008), 66–7.

[27] K. C. Zachariah, 'Religious Denominations of Kerala', *CDS Working Papers* 468 (Thiruvananthapuram: Centre for Development Studies, 2016), 10.

[28] Though of course, communities of Syro-Malabar Catholics exist in much more of the globe than just these main hubs. The parishes of Dubai and Abu Dhabi in the United Arab Emirates, for example, both have large Syro-Malabar congregations.

road, round the corner from a gentlemen's outfitters called 'Urban Geeza!', and a short walk from Europe's largest bus station. To be fair, that description rather undersells the Grade II*-listed church itself. Built for the Jesuits in the gothic style in 1833, just four years after Emancipation, St Ignatius' – as it was then called – set a trend for fine Catholic architecture in the Lancashire town (now city): we will meet several further examples in chapter five. And lest Victorian Preston, the model for Coketown in Dickens' *Hard Times*, conjure up too 'grim oop north' an image, it is worth knowing that the poet, Francis 'Hound of Heaven' Thompson, was baptised at St Ignatius' in 1859. Another, Gerard Manley Hopkins, served as its curate in the 1880s.[29]

For a combination of reasons all too familiar to Catholics in many northern towns and cities – the original Irish Catholic immigrants moving up and out; new immigrants replacing them being non-Christians; declining levels of practice among Catholics as a whole; the costs of upkeeping old churches – St Ignatius' was closed in December 2014 after years of slow decline. By then, it had no resident priest and only one Mass each Sunday; its congregation was, to quote the then Bishop of Lancaster, 'very small and elderly and increasingly could not at all adequately care for the fabric of this church or presbytery'.[30] The following month, however, it was announced that the church would be given over to the northwestern dioceses' thriving Syro-Malabar chaplaincy, established in 2004. St Ignatius' would be rededicated to St Alphonsa of the Immaculate Conception, a twentieth-century Keralan nun whom Benedict XVI canonised in 2008.

---

[29] Michael Hodges, 'Preston – a Rare Catholic Cityscape', *Catholic Herald*, 18 July 2021, <https://catholicherald.co.uk/preston-a-rare-catholic-cityscape/>.

[30] Michael Campbell, 'On the new Syro-Malabar Diocese, Eparch and New Cathedral for Preston!', *The Bishop's Blog*, 1 August 2016, *https://bishopswarbricks.blog/2016/08/*.

This was originally one of two 'personal parishes'[31] erected for the Syro-Malabar community within the Diocese of Lancaster, with another in Blackpool without a church of its own, but using borrowed space in existing parishes (a model, as noted above, used by the Polish parishes in Scotland).[32] In July 2016, the Holy See announced a new eparchy for Britain's large Syro-Malabar diaspora, with St Alphonsa's as its mother church. This is now being turned, slowly but surely, from a 'pre-loved', fixer-upper Anglo-Irish parish into a gleaming Anglo-Indian Cathedral. We have witnessed this metamorphosis ourselves over successive visits: the original plaster statues now bedecked with flowers; Our Lady of Lourdes garlanded with an enormous light-up rosary necklace; each time a different section fenced off and scaffolded for repairs; and – best of all – large, multi-generational congregations, with lots of families and young adults.

While the full Syro-Malabar history in Britain remains to be written, its broadest contours can be summarised like so:

> In the 1950s a small number of Syro-Malabar faithful migrated to the UK for employment purposes. Later, in the 1960s a few medical doctors and their families arrived. By 2000, a large number of nurses and some Information Technology professionals migrated to the

---

[31] 'As a general rule a parish is to be territorial, that is, one which includes all the Christian faithful of a certain territory. When it is expedient, however, personal parishes are to be established determined by reason of the rite, language, or nationality of the Christian faithful of some territory, or even for some other reason' (*Code of Canon Law*, §531). This provision has been rarely used in Britain, though we will see some other examples in chapter five. In the United States, there is a long history of personal parishes. While the fashion for them has waxed and waned over time, they currently appear to be quite in vogue, catering to various liturgical, ethnic, or other ecclesial niches. On this whole topic, see the excellent Tricia Colleen Bruce, *Parish and Place: Making Room for Diversity in the American Catholic Church* (New York: Oxford University Press, 2017).

[32] 'Lancaster: Two Syro-Malabar Catholic parishes established', *Independent Catholic News*, 21 April 2015, <https://www.indcatholicnews.com/news/27248>.

UK… Most of the faithful are young and working families, well-educated professionals that are an asset to the community.[33]

The eparchy estimates the Syro-Malabar population here to be 50,000 and 'steadily increasing due to new immigrations'.[34] Upon its erection, existing provision within dioceses, including the new personal parishes and a patchwork of chaplaincy 'missions' throughout the country, were thence incorporated into it. Since then, more and more have steadily been added. These include a growing number of permanent church buildings, 'surplus' donated by (or bought from) local dioceses: Our Lady Queen of Peace in the Archdiocese of Liverpool, St Mary's and St Wilfrid's in the Diocese of Leeds, St Thomas's (formerly St Joseph's) in the Diocese of Clifton. Alongside these parishes, there are fifty-two 'missions' (i.e., stable congregations with a regular, borrowed place of worship), with a further thirty-three in the works. Ramsgate Abbey, formerly of the Subiaco Congregation of Benedictines, is also now the busy Divine Retreat Centre, run by a Syro-Malabar order of Vincentians.[35] As of March 2024, the eparchy has 69 priests ministering in Britain, hailing from various Indian eparchies and religious orders, and three seminarians of its own in formation.

'Protection and advancement'

Before considering some of Britain's smaller Eastern Catholic communities, it is worth focussing here on quite why these groups need to be considered separately to our other diasporic communities,

---

[33] Martin Thomas Antony, 'Role of Ecclesiastical Structure in the Promotion of Authentic Spirituality among the Diaspora: An Experience from the Evolution of the Syro Malabar Church in the United Kingdom', *Journal of St Thomas Christians* 31/2 (2020), 43–53, at 45.

[34] For this and other information, we are grateful to Fr Mathew Pinakkattu, the Eparchy's Chancellor.

[35] See <https://www.divineuk.org/ramsgate/>. Retreats are offered in English, Malayalam, Tamil, and Konkani. We have elsewhere noted the significance of Britain's Tamil and Konkani (i.e., the primary language in Goa) Catholic communities.

despite a great many commonalities between them. This is not, for example, simply a matter of numbers, dedicated clergy, or infrastructure: the Polish Catholic Missions have plenty of all three, for example. Rather, the difference is at root an ecclesiological one.

Each of the twenty-three Eastern Catholic Churches is not merely a branch of the (Western) Latin Church, but is a *sui juris* Church in its own right. As Robin Gibbons, a British priest of the Melkite Greek Catholic Church, puts it: 'In other words they have their own identity, charism and structure, their liturgical rites are authentic, their customs legitimate, their doctrine sound.'[36] In this vein, Vatican II – a general council of the universal Catholic Church, and not just of the Latin branch of it (as several Eastern Council Fathers were keen to point out)[37] – stressed two important things. The first is this:

> Means should be taken therefore in every part of the world for the protection and advancement of all the individual Churches and, to this end, there should be established parishes and a special hierarchy where the spiritual good of the faithful demands it.

The second:

> Each and every Catholic, as also the baptised of every non-Catholic church or denomination who enters into the fullness of the Catholic communion, must retain his own rite wherever he is, must cherish it and observe it to the best of his ability.[38]

What this means is that, wherever they are in the world, the Eastern Churches and their members have not just a right to exist

---

[36] Robin Gibbons, 'Pride and Prejudice: The Vocation of the Eastern Catholic Churches', *One in Christ* 34/2 (2009), 35–53, at 37–8.

[37] Shaun Blanchard and Stephen Bullivant, *Vatican II: A Very Short Introduction* (Oxford: Oxford University Press, 2023), 5.

[38] *Orientalium Ecclesiarum*, 4.

(cf. 'means… for the protection'), but a duty to flourish ('…and advancement'). And this is true at both the organisational and individual levels. To put it a little roughly, it is not simply that the Eastern Churches themselves are to be 'protected and advanced' in a particular diaspora setting, but the individual members of those Churches need to (be helped to) 'protect and advance' their own specific Eastern Catholicity.[39] Furthermore, all this is not only incumbent on the Eastern Catholics themselves. Rather, there is an expectation that the dominant 'particular Church' – usually, though not necessarily, the Latin one – should be doing what *it* can to help them in this.

Addressing the situation of Eastern Catholic migrants living outside of their Churches' historic homelands – such as Syro-Malabars in Lanarkshire and Lancashire – the Pontifical Council for the Care of Migrants and Itinerant Peoples gives some 'very clear recommendations',[40] including:

> Eastern Rite Catholic migrants, whose numbers are steadily increasing, deserve particular pastoral attention. In their regard we should first of all remember the juridical obligation of the faithful to observe their own rite everywhere insofar as possible, rite being understood as their liturgical, theological, spiritual and disciplinary heritage.[41]

---

[39] Strictly speaking, it is not *impossible* to switch one's membership between different particular Churches – Latin to Ukrainian, or Ukrainian to Latin, say – but it is strictly regulated in canon law. The most common, and administratively easy, way is when marrying a Catholic from a different particular Church, one can opt to join one's spouse's. Children, under the age of 14, in 'Catholicly mixed' marriages can also change. All others require permission from the Holy See, which tends not to be given lightly. See *Code of Canon Law*, §112.

[40] Robin Gibbons, 'The Eastern Catholic Diaspora in Contemporary Europe: Context and Challenges', *Downside Review* 134/4 (2016), 147–60, at 153.

[41] *Erga migrantes caritas Christi* (2004), art. 52. Available online: https://www.vatican.va/roman_curia/pontifical_councils/migrants/documents/rc_pc_migrants_doc_20040514_erga-migrantes-caritas-christi_en.html. Other relevant magisterial texts are helpfully summarized in Catholic Syro-Malabar Eparchy of Great Britain, *The Holy to the Holy Ones: Pastoral Plan 2022–2027*, 27–47. Available online: https://malankaralibrary.com/ImageUpload/cd0fbc70cc1faac4ff74f2ecfb6fae16.pdf.

In reality, however, that 'insofar as possible' often has to do a great deal of heavy lifting. Even where it is possible to worship regularly in one's own rite, other pastoral provision can be harder to sustain. This is especially the case for those with school-age children, whose catechesis and sacramental preparation often, understandably enough, occurs within the local (Latin-rite) parish and school. Where Eastern Catholic parishes or other mission centres exist, alternative arrangements are possible. Some additional rite-specific 'liturgical, theological, spiritual' formation might also be provided, either in regular lay-led small groups, or larger day events or retreats. For example, a key element of the Syro-Malabar Church's global pastoral strategy is the *kudumba kootayma* or Family Unit. As the Eparchy here explains it, these aim:

> ...to build up the Church in view of providing greater pastoral care for families and individuals among the Syro-Malabar faithful in Great Britain. A few families living in a defined area of a Parish/Qurbana centre gather together as a unit to pray and to reflect. A family unit ought to be true expression of communion as well as a means to build up a vibrant parish community. The formation and effective functioning of family units will contribute immensely to the life and growth of the new Eparchy of Great Britain. Family units are nourished by the Word of God and called to remain embedded into the local Church and the universal Church. By maintaining a sincere communion with the priests whom [the] Lord gives to His Church the family units constantly should grow in missionary consciousness, fervour, commitment and zeal. The units thereby will become centres of Christian formation and missionary outreach. The family units consist of families that gather for prayer, Scripture reading, catechesis, and reflection on human and ecclesial matters.

It is true that pastoral vision statements on diocesan (or eparchial) websites do not always perfectly mirror reality. This one, however, seems to be the exception that proves the rule: parish/mission websites and Facebook groups attest to the vitality of the Family Unit scene at the local level.

But all this requires significant resources and organisation, as well as, of course, a sufficient critical mass of committed laity within a particular locale. Britain's Ukrainian and Syro-Malabar eparchies might, at least in some areas of the country, be able to muster a comprehensive pastoral subculture.[42] But even for these, it is not easy. It is all the harder for the much smaller and more stretched groups of Eastern Catholic Churches present in Britain.

Several of these have a semi-permanent British base. The Maronite Church, an ancient Syriac foundation which has never been out of communion with Rome, has a single parish – Our Lady of Lebanon – for the whole of England. This is based in London, accommodated on a 'church-share' basis in a Westminster parish (until recently Our Lady of Sorrows, Paddington; now Our Lady of Lourdes and St Vincent de Paul, Harrow Road). The Melkite Greek Catholic Church, another ancient Holy Land foundation with perhaps 5,000 members in Britain, also comprises a single parish. Theirs is a church-share with an Anglican church in Pimlico, attracting a congregation of 50-100 on Sundays, with perhaps 3-400 at Easter or major feast days. Regular Divine Liturgies also used to be offered in Oxford.[43]

The Belarus Greek Catholic Church possesses its own chapel: an award-winningly beautiful wooden one (the first in London since the Great Fire), built in a traditional Belarusian style, way up the Northern Line at Woodside Park. Small but perfectly formed from rough-hewn timber, its congregation numbered just twelve for the

---

[42] Indeed, note this telling anecdote from a British priest in Nottingham, whose church hosts liturgies for the local Syro-Malabar and Syro-Malankara missions. He once introduced himself to two visiting children as 'the parish priest here'. He received the reply, spoken in a broad East Midlands accent: 'You can't be a priest. You're the wrong colour.'

[43] Thanks to John Shinkwin for his information on this and other matters.

9.30am Divine Liturgy we visited in January 2020. At 11am, the same church hosting the Slovak Greek Catholic Church was filled to overcapacity with around forty-five. This evidently close-knit congregation had a heavy skew towards young adults and families. Of the two people over 60, one had come prepared with a handbag full of KitKats to distract fractious little ones: a real community service in so small and densely packed a room. A young priest, vested magnificently in golden robes and a crown, led a highly ritualised Byzantine Liturgy with great solemnity and precision, with the whole congregation (visiting sociologist and his daughter notwithstanding), children included, knowing precisely when and what to do, sing, or say. Meanwhile his homily, in Slovakian, was delivered extempore in a folksy style, with much waving and smiling at toddlers. Proof, if proof were needed, that traditional liturgy and 'being pastoral' is not a zero-sum game.

This kind of 'pan-Eastern' sharing – i.e. the Belarusians sharing their church with a (larger) Slovak congregation – is quite common among Britain's Eastern Catholics. The Melkite parish priest is, in fact, actually a Maronite priest with bi-ritual faculties. An Easter Liturgy celebrated by a visiting Romanian Greek chaplain might well be attended by other Byzantine-rite Catholics celebrating *Pascha* on that day.[44] In 2023, the Ukrainian Cathedral hosted London's Hungarian Greek community for the visit of their Church's head, Metropolitan Fülöp Kocsis, with Hungarian, Ukrainian, Melkite, Belarussian, and Romanian clergy all concelebrating. And on a more ongoing basis, Syro-Malabars and Syro-Malankaras, who share a common vernacular in Malayalam, frequently worship together. These might alternate between liturgical rites (the former is East Syriac, the latter West Syriac, for those interested), depending on

---

[44] One of us attended just such a Liturgy in Oxford in 2022, held at St Benet's Hall, and attended by Romanian, Melkite, and Ukrainian Greek Catholics, plus various curious Latin-riters.

clergy availability. Over time, as numbers grow and/or organisation improves, these congregations might split. We visited one regular Syro-Malankara community, hosted by a Nottingham parish, that had amicably 'consciously decoupled' from a larger Syro-Malabar congregation in this way. (Incidentally, this is a fine example of a Latin-rite parish and an Eastern Catholic congregation combining to provide 'means... for the protection and advancement' of *another* Eastern Catholic congregation in a given diaspora locale.) As Syro-Malankara groups grow and go their own way, one suspects they may well become Britain's third eparchy.

These examples from our fieldwork represent fewer than a third of the world's Eastern Catholic Churches. Even some of these more prominent examples, as we have seen, exist in only a small and relatively precarious way in Britain, at least in terms of pastoral organisation (actual numbers, spread over the whole of Britain, may in some cases be rather larger than their institutional footprint suggests). Only a very few have realistic prospects of the kind of full and independent flourishing aspired to in the Church documents. Nevertheless, it is this aspiration which marks a significant difference, in principle, between Eastern Catholics and those from the other diasporic communities. As is clear from the above, the Eastern Catholic churches in Britain should ideally, 'insofar as possible', have an independent and autonomous footing within the wider Catholic landscape: existing *alongside*, rather than within, the Latin Church. Such an existence is certainly possible for Eastern Catholic Churches in western diaspora settings: the Maronite Church in Australia, or the Ukrainian Church in parts of America and Canada, are good examples of what is possible. And at least in certain places here, something approximating it is possible for Syro-Malabar and Ukrainian Catholics too.

By contrast, at least as far as the dioceses are concerned, the primary role of Britain's (non-Eastern) ethnic, linguistic, and/or migrant chaplaincies is a kind of bridging one. Masses in Lithuanian, Tagalog, or Shona are a means to the ultimate end of 'integrating' immigrants into existing parish structures.[45] Of course, 'integration' can be interpreted in different ways. However it is meant, it is often understood as implying cultural assimilation, and erasure of difference. This might seem both a bit rich, and indeed counterproductive, not least when the diasporic communities exhibit much higher levels of commitment and devotion than do the normal (and normative) parish cultures into which they are supposed to be absorbed. Furthermore, parishes *already* offer a range of liturgical offerings catering to different groups (e.g., a family Mass, with children's liturgy; an early Sunday 'sports Mass' for those with games to get to), or liturgical preferences (folk Mass with guitars, high Mass with organ and full choir, a short and sweet evening Mass with minimal music), often with congregations at least partly drawn from outside of the parish. Yet no bishop dares suggest that these parishes are dis-integrated because of it. Indeed, a Catholic parish is *supposed* to be a 'community of communities' (*Evangelii Gaudium*, 28). Accordingly, a more positive framing might be to view 'integration' as involving a more permanent embedding of diasporic communities themselves, along with their devotions, customs, lay groups, and (where possible) regular vernacular Masses, into what is considered 'the normal parish offering'. In practice, a great deal of this already goes on in British churches.

Conclusion

This chapter attempts to give no more than an *impression* of all that is presently going on in Britain's Catholic diasporic and/or Eastern Catholic liturgical communities. These groups are rarely mentioned in the Catholic press and, with a few notable exceptions – the Poles most obviously – there has been precious little research done on any of them. Even those 'in', or at least well acquainted with, one such group may well have little awareness of (m)any of the others.

---

[45] On this, see Gray and Ryan, 'Migrant chaplaincy'; Trzebiatowska, 'Easyjet Priest'.

Collectively, these groups represent a significant segment of British Catholicism's present – one that it is certainly undercounted in official church statistics.[46] More to the point, there are strong reasons for thinking that they will contribute disproportionately to its future too. This is so for two reasons. Firstly and most obviously, immigration will continue. This may well be a different mix to that of recent decades, presumably including fewer from the EU, but will still include large numbers of Catholics. The NHS's appetite for Filipino and Indian doctors and nurses, for example, shows little signs of being sated any time soon.[47] Secondly, there is a wealth of evidence suggesting that a) members of close-knit congregations with high average levels of commitment tend to galvanise each other, in a kind of virtuous circle;[48] and b) children raised in those environments, and by those kinds of parents, are most likely to retain at least some of this religious zeal into adulthood themselves.[49] Such inter-generational religious transmission is a very long way from being perfect. But even so, the next generation of practising British Catholic adults, say twenty or thirty years from now, will surely include more than its fair share of second-generation immigrants. And so too will the seminaries.

---

[46] This is so for two main reasons. The first is that the kinds of ethnic/linguistic congregations considered here often sit outside of dioceses' usual parish-based system of counting and recording. It is also the case that figures for the Ukrainian and Syro-Malabar eparchies (if they collect them) are not included in the annual England and Wales datasets assembled by the Bishops' Conference. It may be that some of the latter's congregations end up included in the corresponding (Latin) diocesan counts, but again, it is hard to know how systematically this is done, if it all.

[47] Álvaro Alonso-Garbayo and Jill Maben, 'Internationally Recruited Nurses from India and the Philippines in the United Kingdom: The Decision to Emigrate', *Human Resources for Health* 7/37 (2009), 1–11.

[48] Samuel Stroope, 'Social Networks and Religion: The Role of Congregational Social Embeddedness in Religious Belief and Practice', *Sociology of Religion* 73/3 (2012), 273–98; Matthew Facciani and Matthew E. Brashears 'Sacred Alters: The Effects of Ego Network Structure on Religious and Political Beliefs', *Socius* 5 (2019), 1–16.

[49] For a small selection of the research undergirding this, see the Introduction, footnote 24.

4. University chaplaincies and CathSocs

Late one wet January afternoon after the Thursday lunchtime Mass, ten or so university students meet in the nearest Wetherspoons for 'Book Club'. Following burgers, fish and chips, and a festively apt haggis, neeps, and tatties, and just in time for the second pint, these members of a London CathSoc[1] delve into *The Love That Is God* by Frederick Christian Bauerschmidt. Led by Fr Jake,[2] the Catholic chaplain, students were invited to bring their own copy of the book and follow along as a member of the group read out the text. Frequent pauses were made for questions, commentary, or clarification of concepts by students and chaplains alike. This title was the second in the series of the 'Book Club' that academic year, with the first having been *Another Sort of Learning* by James V. Schall SJ. This new title was an opportunity to explore 'the radical claim of Christianity that God is love, which is far more extraordinary than probably most of us… take it as being now because we've heard it… trivialised', or because preachers haven't effectively communicated it, but that rather it should be understood as the 'explosive root' of our Faith.[3] What was needed was a re-sensitisation to the claims of Christianity for a culture that presumed it already knew and understood its historic religion.

The contrast of sitting in a profane, ostensibly godless place talking about ultimate things, and the ways in which they made a

---

[1] The terms 'CathSoc' (Catholic Society) and 'chaplaincy' will be used from here interchangeably unless differentiation is warranted
[2] Names given to chaplains and students in this chapter are pseudonyms.
[3] Frederick C. Bauerschmidt, *The Love That Is God: An Invitation to Christian Faith* (Grand Rapids, MI: Eerdmans, 2020), 1.

claim on us, was not lost on me[4] as I sat and listened to the conversation. It was striking to consider how the students were engaging in metaphysical discussions in the most ordinary of places. What is more, they had carved not an insignificant amount of time out of their day to contemplate these things. Fr Jake described how, 'faith is not just one more fact about the world, but rather that faith is a worldview, and so it informs the way that we… understand… everything we encounter'. As we sat on beer-stained seats, around three or four awkwardly conjoined tables, here we were trying to craft a 'well-thought-through worldview'. Paul asked about how we can defend objective morality; Alex shared about the inconsistencies of tolerance culture; Zoe dwelt on the notion that love empowers us to live with one another in society despite our differences. The fundamental topics of where values come from, what nature consists of, and how – with this knowledge – we might have a vision for human flourishing, emerged out of the discussion. The existence of Book Club affirmed the right of the students to *ask* about the Faith. When I asked what the importance of this intellectual formation was, 'Father' – as he was universally called, whether in person or on WhatsApp – commissioned all of us to use it to 'contribute to society… a more coherent way of thinking', and to consider on a personal level, 'why am I doing what I'm doing?', that we might 'enable other people to ask that question of themselves and give them a potentially more sensible answer they might have [received] otherwise'. Evangelisation can begin without use of explicitly Christian language, he said, as having conversations with others about what they desire, how they experience internal conflicts or their own woundedness, and how healing could be possible, were good segues into our Faith.

This snapshot intends to provide a window into the inner workings of one university chaplaincy, where students were being

[4] BD.

prepared for Christian mission. The students that attended Book Club were frequent – often daily – Mass-goers and willingly identified as Catholic, firmly constituting a group attracting increased sociological attention in recent years: 'highly religious young Catholics'.[5]

The majority of the research for this chapter was completed as part of a doctoral project exploring the contribution of university chaplaincies to Catholicism in the UK.[6] It focussed mainly on a single field site – a Russell Group university in central London – between May 2021 and September 2022. Given its location, this university had close links to a wider Catholic student world, most notably via Newman House, the chaplaincy residence for students enrolled at London universities. Additional fieldwork has been undertaken at two other institutions in the East of England and in Northern Ireland.[7] Our focus is on regular attendees to chaplaincy/CathSoc events.

Entering these groups, being Catholic was vital for getting students to be relaxed about talking about their faith with me. I was affectionately nicknamed 'the mole', yet students also knew I was 'on their side'. Regular attendance at Mass, enthusiastically singing along with the *Missa De Angelis*, and carrying rosary beads in my handbag allowed people to open up. As with most student environments, the turnover of people can be quite high. Sometimes people popped into Mass once, or just came for the free lunch a

---

[5] José P. Coutinho, Brian Conway, and Siniša Zrinščak, 'Special issue—Highly Religious Young Catholics', *Sociology Compass* 17/7 (2023), e13118.

[6] In addition to this dedicated fieldwork by BD, all three of this book's authors have spent significant amounts of time over the past two decades at a wide range of British universities – as undergraduates, postgraduates, academic or chaplaincy staff, and visiting speakers. These experiences have also contributed to the perspectives we offer here.

[7] The nuance that Irish/Northern Irish Catholicism requires cannot be explored here, and as such will not be covered in any detail. As it is beyond the scope of this chapter, these themes will be explored in separate publications. The primary focus for this volume is Britain.

few times. This meant that often I would have to introduce myself to the new faces, lest they think I was officially 'one of them'. Many students, however, were so regular that they were part of the furniture, demonstrating that the chaplaincy was vital to their everyday living. Students often jokingly asked if I was Catholic, saying, 'well, why else would you be researching us?', as if this topic was too niche for even the most interested of outsiders. This gets at the heart of this research: trying to map out where the growth is happening, because perhaps it is too much of a well-kept secret. This is despite – or maybe because - we know anecdotally that in certain pockets, levels of engagement are nothing short of impressive.

The London group had access to two chapels across their campuses. The main chapel had a great regal feel, heavily decorated with red and gold walls, with altar rails, both traditional and stand-alone altars, an inbuilt choir and accompanying organ towards the back of the chapel, and several, long, wooden, red-cushioned benches, perhaps enough to fit 300 people. Closer to the altar were horizontally aligned benches. Despite different Christian groups using this space, at first glance, it wasn't obvious that this wasn't already a Catholic chapel. (One student once humorously commented to me that they needed to increase the space between the benches as the Anglicans didn't need extra floor space to kneel as Catholics did.) Stained glass memorials of saints lined the chapel walls, an unavoidable reference to Christian tradition and its religious and spiritual legacy. Passers-by often popped in either to put a face to the dulcet tones of the female cantor rehearsing the Gregorian chant chosen for Mass as it soared through the university corridors, or simply to look inside a place that, without the doors being opened, would have remained unnoticed. For all anyone knew, behind the floor-to-ceiling imposing, dark wooden doors could have been just another lecture theatre or conference facility. The Thursday lunchtime Masses were well-attended generally, encouraged perhaps by the promise of a free lunch which consisted of self-assembled sandwiches (bagels, French baguettes, ham, cheese), the odd bag of salad leaves, pots of hummus, culminating in flapjacks and chocolate brownies for an afternoon treat. A core group of students were guaranteed to turn up each week, appearing to take their Thursday attendance as seriously as their Sunday. A quasi-parish formed, fully staffed with musicians, altar servers, and readers. On the odd occasion that 'Father' was running late, we made ourselves useful, and, following the CathSoc president's lead, said a Rosary. The liturgical style of the weekly Masses were *novus ordo*, solemn, and beautiful. Every person consciously contributed to the ambient silence. Conversations in the chapel were kept to the strictly necessary things: questions like, 'would you like to read?', 'do you need a hymn book?'. It could never be said that Mass was not taken seriously, but also never without joy.

In a homily at Mass on one Lenten lunchtime, Fr Jake expounded upon the First Reading that day, Deuteronomy 30.15-20, a passage where Moses encourages the people to choose life in obedience to God in order to reach the land that had been promised for them. Reminded of the 1990s classic, *Trainspotting*, Father challenged the students to enter into the penitential season consciously, encouraging them – as adults – to take responsibility and not see this solely as another season for a chocolate or crisp fast. He offered an updated, duly sanitised version of a monologue from the recent sequel, *T2 Trainspotting*, from the character Mark Renton (played by Ewan McGregor) on the danger of being a passive participant in modern culture. He explained that 'the culture' is comprised of little decisions:

> There are a *whole host* of choices that each of us make, without even realising it. They're what we might call the choices of the culture, the things our culture values, and which without even having to think about, we can automatically prioritise.

But *our* culture has ceased to be Christian, and the cultural tide will not take us where we need to go. So, we need to *really* choose, we need to get *really* conscious. If you don't choose, the culture will choose for you, and they're not going to be good choices. You will not be choosing life and not to choose life is to choose something else instead. There is only one other option. And the choice not to choose? Well, that's the choice itself and it does not lead to life.

The students were encouraged prayerfully and carefully to identify the godless forces of contemporary life that were being thrust upon them, even in the most mundane ways. Here the necessity of the intellectual (the extent that students understand the faith) and social (the extent to which this faith is shared and discussed with others) formation with personal or human formation became clear. As the students opted into Catholicism as a way of life, and as more than 'just' a conservative worldview, they were reminded of the costs that may be accrued in this valley of tears:

> Moses tells us the choices that lead to life: love of the Lord, living in this love, and keeping his commandments. ... [W]hen we look at what we really value, when we look at what *really* motivates us, we'll see what we suffer for and therefore what we love. And we cannot love Jesus and reject his Cross. The two cannot be separated, because Christian love is cross-shaped. ... And there comes a time when we need to choose greater things to love, greater things to suffer for. To choose to suffer for that which truly gives life, the victory over sin, not just that over a sporting appointment or a rival in class. So then, this Lent, I'd invite you to look at all that you do, and if you're going to keep on doing [it], make sure to choose it. ... Make prayer the place where you're passive, where you're open to whatever God may ask of you, but in the rest of your life, be active. ... And then perhaps each of us might

begin to choose better. .... Choose life. Choose love. Choose God. Embrace the Cross or pay a much worse cost.

The underlying sense here of personal responsibility rings through religious sentiment, as the students were encouraged to manage their own actions and form their identities. The future of Catholicism, in many ways, does rest on their shoulders to the extent that they can suffer for truth and goodness. This sense of the students *contra mundum* did not primarily intend to reflect their own perception of social marginality (due to unpopular beliefs and practices) but was for the *sake* of the world. Their perception was that, when – and not if – society realises the errors of its ways, they will be grateful that the Church held fast to truth and reason, and this would be worth any misunderstanding or opposition that they may face from others now. Essentially, the university was mission territory. The keenness to establish or continue a faith that is 'just Catholic' relies on these above characteristics. This attribution was deliberately intended to be apolitical and non-partisan, in the hope of transcending contemporary debates about how best to embody Catholicism. The current politicisation of the faith was believed to be an unhelpful distraction, capable of disillusioning both insiders and outsiders.

Underlying this sensibility – whether conscious or not – was an 'ought' that appeared to direct the essence of these groups: accessing the Divine Life. The Catholic identity was accountable to a real 'other' – one superior to any other temporal identity (including family backgrounds, culture, ethnic makeup, gender, class etc.). This was maintained by the union of spirituality with religion – the interplay of personal mystical experience and traditional authority. In short, the more the students became aware of their highest and true – that is to say, God-given – identity by association in the group, the more they used their religious and spiritual capital to invest in their lives of faith.

Zoe, a PhD student, after weathering the breakup of a romantic relationship, said she had experienced 'an absolute deluge of grace', that led her to start attending Adoration of the Blessed Sacrament weekly, and increasing her Mass attendance to more than her Sunday obligation: practices that, until recently, she would have seen as only done by 'weirdos'. Eventually, she felt the Lord calling her to reconsider the possibility of religious life and made a deal with the Lord to give her three months to make her vocation clear. She had planned to:

> Metaphorically walk through the [religious life] door and close it, not lock it, but close it… and then, at the end of those three months, when I know that it's not for me, because You [God] have shown me that it's not for me, I will go and find some lovely postgrad with a new influx of students in September, some nice… Catholic PhD student who I can go and marry. … That was my plan. You know, maybe… the new term will bring in someone cute, right? And in the meantime, I'll give you three months. The Lord was like, 'Great! Running with it!'

By the end of three months, she said: 'three priests had independently mentioned [a specific] community to me, and only one knew I was discerning'. She realised she had to explore this avenue seriously despite her initial hesitancy. Not too long before this, Zoe had enrolled on a student RCIA course – not because she needed to get baptised, but because she wanted to study Church teaching systematically to understand it for herself. As the Faith came to mean more to her, she found herself rearranging her weekly schedule to fit in daily Mass and attending more CathSoc events, as she discovered that its members were 'normal'. Activities that fit this description included frequent daily Mass attendance, knowing the difference between Bible Study and *Lectio Divina* (and using the Latin term in a casual and unaffected way), or fangirling over particular saints,[8] just to give a few examples of this subculture. It was also 'normal' to be trying out religious vocations. By the time I came to leave the London group in the summer of 2022, one woman had paused studies to join a convent the previous Christmas, a man and a woman were about to enter religious life at the end of the summer following the completion of their degrees, and another was hoping to begin seminary after graduation which required another two year wait. And those were the ones that were *publicly* discerning.

The perpetuation of the Catholic lens is precisely the *raison d'être* of the university chaplaincy. Furthermore, human beings are, as St Thomas Aquinas quotes approvingly from Aristotle, 'social animals'.[9] Our own views, beliefs, tastes and actions are constantly influenced by those around us, in all kinds of subtle ways: 'Humans are not exactly lemmings, but they are easily influenced by the statements and deeds of others.'[10] And this is as true of religious believing, behaving and belonging as it is of, say, political convictions, moral outlook or fashion sense. Thus, as Pope Francis put it in his maiden encyclical, *Lumen Fidei*: 'We can respond in the singular – "I believe" – only because we are part of a greater fellowship, only because we also say "We believe".'[11] For our Catholic students, the impulse to understand the faith more deeply,

---

[8] On this theme, another of us overheard 'three normal 17ish girls' (as per the fieldwork notes) at Youth 2000's summer festival in Walsingham comparing their friends' and siblings' confirmation saints. These included such traditional favourites as Philomena, Maximilian, Raphael, and Thérèse. The following interjection was typical: 'Oh, I *love* her! I wish I had Thérèse as my middle name.' On this theme, see also Katherine A. Dugan '"St Gemma Is My Girl!": Devotional Practices among Millennial Catholics and the Making of Contemporary Catholic Saints', *American Catholic Studies*, 127/4 (2016), 1–21.

[9] Thomas Aquinas, *Summa theologiae*, II-I, q. 95, a. 4.

[10] Richard H. Thaler and Cass R. Sunstein, *Nudge: Improving Decisions about Health, Wealth, and Happiness* (New Haven CT: Yale University Press, 2008), Chapter 3.

[11] Pope Francis, *Lumen Fidei*, 39, available online: <https://www.vatican.va/content/francesco/en/encyclicals/documents/papa-francesco_20130629_enciclica-lumen-fidei.html>. The document was promulgated by Pope Francis, but had already been substantially drafted by Pope Benedict XVI prior to his retirement. This particular passage has a definite 'Benedictine' ring to it, it must be said.

whether formally or over a pint, was ever-present. And it was the CathSoc environment that *created the conditions for the possibility* to believe that we were created out of love, made for happiness, that life was ultimately good and meaningful, that sins could be forgiven, suffering could be redemptive, and that we were made for a world beyond this one. All of this lent itself to the notion that the Catholic worldview could indeed be true.

Courses were a common part of chaplaincy life. The university in the East of England used Fr Stephen Wang's popular Sycamore programme, while the London group regularly availed themselves of those from the US-based Ascension Press. Attendance at Bible studies throughout the year were often fully subscribed. These usually welcomed twelve students across a Microsoft Teams screen and lasted for around a term, allowing students to take a 'deep dive' into a topic of the Faith that they were ostensibly already quite familiar with. When I first joined the London group, they were beginning a study called, 'A Biblical Walk through the Mass', devised by Edward Sri. On Teams, this course was led by two students, with Fr Jake and the lay chaplain Dan on hand to answer any complex questions. Ahead of the discussion groups, students were encouraged to read a chapter from the set text, answer questions in the workbook, and watch the video recordings of lectures given by the enthusiastic Sri. This was a chance to discuss some of the deeper questions about the symbolism behind the Mass and trace the specific line of ritual from the Jewish tradition. Perhaps in part because of the nature of the sample, members of the group often raised insightful questions and engaged in great discussions. Together they created an environment where it was safe to interrogate assumptions. It was fascinating to observe the discussions of students as the proverbial penny seemed to drop for many of them over the nine or so weeks of the course. By virtue of being young adults as well, the students were keen to find out what they believed about the world, who they might associate with, and what goals could they orientate their lives towards. The confidence displayed by the chaplains reinforced the notion of the internal coherence of Catholicism – that everything does make sense and points back directly to Christ whilst also accounting for mystery.

Tom, a medical student, chatted with me over Zoom about the significance of another Wednesday night Bible Study titled 'Unlocking the Mystery of the Bible'. 'Not being very good at reading the Bible' on his own, having only a basic understanding, he enrolled on this course to improve his chances of engaging with it. Following a recommendation from the chaplains, Tom purchased the *Didache Bible* which contains extensive references to the Catechism and important notes on historical and literary context.[12] This was nothing less than a 'game changer' for him. Tom also described his excitement at the ability of CathSoc to increase numbers too at the Bible Studies. Grinning, he said, it was a 'real surprise' to him to realise that the Catholic community at the university was 'going strong', much stronger than he had anticipated before he joined, and in an environment that he conceded was 'not the most religious place'. He always felt comfortable asking questions as the chaplaincy atmosphere was considered safe and that no question was too stupid to bring to the group. One of many 'realisation' moments for Tom in his faith had been understanding certain familiar phrases from Scripture. Studying the agony in the garden, he began to understand the gravity of the temptation Jesus suffered:

> I was like, '*Woah*!' you know, hang on a minute because, is [Jesus] trying to… is he being tempted of getting away from the crucifixion… and the ultimate sacrifice? Or, but, then it's almost like he realises mid-sentence that, 'oh, hang on. This is… not part of the… script. So, I've got to… get myself back on track'. So, I never thought of that.

---

[12] *The Didache Bible: with Commentaries Based on the Catechism of the Catholic Church* (San Francisco, CA: Ignatius Press, 2015).

Tom valued the opportunity to explore the Bible with his CathSoc peers and begin to see for the first time things that he thought were already part of his stock of knowledge.

Student Catholicism

Despite a reasonable amount of recent research into 'student religion' in Britain, Catholic university chaplaincies have not attracted extensive investigation. This is a shame, given the many good – and sociologically very interesting – things happening on campuses today. The critical few years that have come to represent the 'university experience' often have an outsized effect over the rest of a person's religious life. University can act as the 'make or break' moment for a young adult's faith. Some anthropologists have examined the relationship between the university and rites of passage, particularly with respect to 'status change and identity challenge'.[13] CathSocs on campus are well-placed to offer a strong identity when vulnerabilities may be high, and students feel an acute need to establish themselves. We know that the role of university is crucial in the formation of other Christian groups. Extensive studies have been conducted recruiting from a broad range of denominations to understanding the place and role of faith provision on campuses.[14] Further, other sociologists have found the weight of university to be particularly formative in the lives of practising Christians.[15] Chaplaincy generally is considered to be a 'sector' ministry, meaning it forms one (smallish) part of the Church's mission, unlike parish ministry which is the most regular form of organised participation. As mentioned in chapter two,

---

[13] Edward Dutton, *Meeting Jesus at University: Rites of Passage and Student Evangelicals* (Farnham: Ashgate, 2008), 4.

[14] Matthew Guest, Kristin Aune, Sonya Sharma, and Rob Warner, *Christianity and the University Experience: Understanding Student Faith* (London: Continuum, 2013).

[15] Anna Strahn, *Aliens and Strangers? The Struggle for Coherence in the Everyday Lives of Evangelicals* (Oxford: Oxford University Press, 2015), 13.

chaplaincy is one example of a para-ministry, providing adaptive, specialist support to a particular demographic. 'Para' in this context means 'alongside' or 'beside' and relates to the need for spiritual support outside of – and/or in addition to - the places we might have traditionally expected it.

Across the Atlantic, the Fellowship of Catholic University Students – or FOCUS – has been the subject of research, exploring the peer ministry programme that it provides on campuses to current students.[16] FOCUS trains recent graduates to serve on university campuses and 'win, build, and send' students for Christ. Through prioritising personal prayer and establishing a meaningful relationship with God, this initiative foregrounds evangelisation as Catholicism's *sine qua non*, and works hard to make not just the Faith but also its adherents attractive. In essence, they understand that the medium is as important as the message. Again, on the American scene, other studies have shown students' desire to transform their environments by examining the basic intellectual assumptions of wider secular society.[17] Rather than creating a false tension between academic and spiritual needs, Catholic students and chaplaincies worked hard to change perceptions of what the Faith actually is. This was found to have a twofold effect: bolster the students' own faith, and engage with the sceptics. However, for those courageous enough, this was a balancing act: at one extreme, yielding to the relativism that pervades modern university campuses, and the other, becoming insular, isolated, and defensive towards those who are confused, earnestly searching, and spiritually hungry. These issues are not limited either to the North Atlantic

---

[16] Katherine Dugan, *Millennial Missionaries: How a Group of Young Catholics is Trying to Make Catholicism Cool* (New York: Oxford University Press, 2009). FOCUS is primarily based in the USA, but they did have a short spell in England in the 2010s and are currently based at various locations on the island of Ireland.

[17] Colleen Carroll, *The New Faithful: Why Young Adults are Embracing Christian Orthodoxy* (Chicago, IL: Loyola Press, 2002).

as research on highly religious young Catholics is emerging from places as diverse as Northern Ireland, France, Italy, Croatia, Spain, Mexico, and South Korea.[18]

Closer to home, previous research into British campus Catholicism has revealed the potential for Catholic groups to be 'pockets of vitality' in places where, in addition to a weekly Mass schedule, a priest chaplain may, for example, have a presbytery or parish hall that can be an extension of the chaplaincy building, allowing the community to continue to meet informally and foster relationships.[19] This was certainly the case with the London and the East of England chaplaincies, as priests had additional responsibilities alongside their ministry to students. In such circumstances, the priest can act as a point of continuity in students' faith lives. It has also been noted that some students struggled to adjust to the new 'hostile' environment that was the secular university after having received an education in Catholic institutions or growing up in a less secular part of the world.[20] For the students I encountered though, they were aware that choosing to be Catholic automatically placed them in a socially marginal position. Andrew, for example, 'absolutely' felt this minority status:

---

[18] Highly religious young Catholics in Northern Ireland: Renewing the Catholic Landscape? *Sociology Compass*, e13065; Luca Bossi, Loris Botto, Roberta Ricucci, 'Between Research and Revival: Emerging Trends among Highly Religious Young Catholics in Italy', *Sociology Compass* 17 (2023), e13076; Fabio Bolzonar, 'Conservative Catholicism versus social Catholicism? Contrasting Patterns in the Political Engagement of Highly Religious Young Catholics in France and Italy' *Sociology Compass*, 17/7 (2023), e13092; Željko Boneta and Marko Mrakovčić, 'Religiosity as a Predictor of Students' Political Attitudes', *Sociology Compass* 17(7) (2023), e13090; Joseba García Martín, Cecilia Delgado-Molina, and Mar Griera, "'I'm Going to Do Battle... I'm Going to Do Some Good". Biographical Trajectories, Moral Politics, and Public Engagement among Highly Religious Young Catholics in Spain and Mexico', *Sociology Compass* 17/7 (2023), e13091; Kyuhyun Jung and Seil Oh, 'Enchanted Companionship of Korean Catholic Youth Amid Compressed Individualisation', *Sociology Compass* 17(7), e13082.

[19] Guest et al., *Christianity and the University Experience*, 139.

[20] Peter McGrail and John Sullivan, *Dancing on the Edge: Chaplaincy, Church, and Higher Education* (Chelmsford: Matthew James Publishing, 2007), 24.

> Already as Catholics we're [a] minority in the UK. But practising Catholics... practising religious people form a small part of what statistics say are the religious people. And then even amongst practising like... weekly churchgoers, maybe not everyone agrees with everything the Church teaches.

But for others, being an international student helped them to understand their native country's relationship to the Faith in a new light. Having always felt 'good' and never homesick in England, Tina reflected on one cultural shift that surprised her upon arriving here for her studies:

> I would say the... biggest difference is to arrive in a country where you... notice you're not the main religion. ... Because again, as dechristianised [as] France can be, you just take it for granted. You still are the main religion, whether people are practising or not, [it's] just what it is. It's... not questioned that much yet, I hope! But yeah, and you arrive here, and I think because people are in [a] minority, they're so different. And I really liked the fact that the English Catholics were a lot more outgoing, and conquering, if I may... because, you know, they couldn't rely on this position. They were the minorities, so they had to go and look out for people.

Tina concluded that she thought the 'English atmosphere was a lot more welcoming and tolerant towards religion' generally: 'France has got this very unhealthy and weird relation to religion. So, unless you're in a Catholic school – where, of course, you're in a friendly environment - otherwise those people *hate* to hear talk about religion. This is very uncomfortable.'

The large majority of them were 'out' (a phrase often used) as Catholic to their non-Catholic friends, while maintaining strong friendships despite a difference in worldviews. This is a point worth stressing, lest it be feared that a strong CathSoc *esprit de corps* necessarily breeds insularity or sectarianism. Having moved from India to the East of England university, Trent was pleasantly surprised with the support he received for practising a faith in the UK. He described how his friends showed deference when he hung out with them:

> BD: Do your [non-chaplaincy] friends know that you're Catholic? Are you quite open about that?
> Trent: They know I'm Catholic, and yeah, even they sometimes be careful around me, watch their talk and how to behave and all that. So, I think that is good, they respect that.

Jacob, too, found that whilst he was publicly religious, most friends don't see this as his defining characteristic. When asked if being Catholic was something that his friends knew about, he noted:

> Yeah, yeah, they do… Surprisingly, a lot of people forget about it. I mean, I just don't speak about it too much in front of them. But I do anytime something related to the topic happens, [and] somebody asks if I'm religious or anything like that, and I'll say, 'yeah, yeah I'm Catholic'. They always… tend to forget.

Formative Experiences

As is well documented, parents' religious habits are the single biggest influence on the likelihood of young adults continuing or ceasing practice whilst at university. Those who experience religion positively, coupled with good parental relations, are more likely to attend on their own terms. In fact, the latest research in this field suggests that it is parents that exert the single biggest influence over their offspring's receptivity to the Faith, more than any other institutional or social system (e.g., religious congregations, grandparents, family friends, youth workers, schools).[21] That said, parents are not the sole determiners of their children's religious lives, as is the case with other areas. Rather, sociologists understand that 'religious parents today represent one link in an ongoing, interactive chain of social reproduction and transformation in which all participants involved are the recipients, evaluators, and agents of transmission. The paths and trajectories that such a process can take are dynamic and layered.'[22] To 'opt in' requires the 'religious restraint' of the parents, in the hope of allowing for 'intrinsic commitment' (personal conviction) on the part of children and teens as they age and mature.[23]

When PhD student, Joanna, was growing up 'everyone [she] knew was Catholic', which she attributed to being raised in a certain area of eastern Canada with historically high levels of immigration from Ireland and strong influences from Quebec:

> All my friends went because they all came from a school. So, it was very... like, not all of them were practising, and it wasn't really until high school when I realised like, 'oh, okay, maybe we're a bit different that we actually go to church every week'. But I would never, even now, I wouldn't say that we're like... super practising in the sense where I know... people who[se]... whole family say the Rosary together every night... like, I aspire to that kind of thing, but that wasn't my... upbringing. No, I'm envious [of those that had that upbringing], but that was not mine. Mainly because I don't enjoy saying the Rosary and I wish I did.

---

[21] E.g., Vern L. Bengtson, Norella M. Putney, and Susan Cannon Harris, *Families and Faith: How Religion is Passed down across Generations* (Oxford: Oxford University Press, 2013); Christian Smith and Amy Adamczyk *Handing Down the Faith: How Parents Pass Their Religion on to the Next Generation* (New York: Oxford University Press, 2020).

[22] Smith and Adamczyk, *Handing Down the Faith*, 221.

[23] Ilana M. Horwitz, *God, Grades and Graduation: Religion's Surprising Impact on Academic Success* (New York: Oxford University Press, 2022), 40.

As I probed further to see if she saw herself as particularly religious, she reflected that she did not see herself as either extreme or lukewarm. Interestingly, she linked her (and her siblings') continued religiosity to their parents' 'hands off' approach. This was characterised by strong boundaries, such as kneeling at the bedside before sleep and obligatory Sunday Mass attendance (including when on holiday), and a confident openness, which meant that she never felt that the faith was 'shoved down [their] throats':

> I knew I could ask [my parents] anything... Dad was always, like, 'God gave you a brain, so it's good to question things... and pray and kind of seek answers yourself too'. He was never someone to be, like, 'just blindly follow what a priest says', because he's known some terrible priests and known some, like, stupid priests because they're human and they're flawed the same way anyone is. And I think that was helpful to know that.

For others, faith development was a largely solo venture that did not coincide with that of their parents. Jacek, an undergraduate computer science student, despite being baptised as an infant in Poland, discovered faith during the Covid-19 lockdown after becoming dissatisfied with the atheistic worldview:

> My parents weren't exactly very religious, so I would never really actually be taken to church outside of like, maybe Easter and Christmas. And my family was... quite atheistic, and I kind of, you know, I guess, identified myself as atheist because I didn't really go to church until I was like 16 or 17, when... I started thinking about it more philosophically and came to the conclusion that [atheism] just doesn't really answer most questions for me, and that there has to be something more.

He described that he felt like a 'closeted Catholic' to his family, as he could not anticipate how supportive or not they might have been. Attending an Easter baskets blessing one Holy Saturday,[24] however, served as an opportunity for Jacek to begin to consider how he might disclose his new-found faith to his mother. Visiting the church ahead of attending Mass for what he thought would be a 'fun, family activity' was a 'nice segue' to ask his mother's blessing for his (re)conversion.

Choosing My Religion

Some religious young adults lose their faith at university, or else it, often unintentionally, gradually slides down the list of priorities. Other, hitherto non-religious teens and twenty-somethings find faith, or else, much to their (and their families') surprise, find a low-level cultural Catholicism suddenly spark into flame. Having met and spoken to a wide variety of students throughout this project, and indeed having known many others separate to it, we can affirm that there is no universal trend. However, for those that *do* embrace religion at university, the level of saliency they attribute to it is striking. This is, of course, another example of the 'creative minority effect' set out in the Introduction. If these young adults' religiosity *wasn't* important to them, they wouldn't (perhaps even couldn't) be religious at all. And this receives social reinforcement from hanging out with others in a similar situation. For interesting social psychological reasons, this situation can create a mutually reinforcing cycle. In effect, many CathSoc members become 'radicalised': experimenting with mantillas, praying the rosary, considering vocations, googling 'NFP'.

Understood in this way, CathSocs do two main important things. First, they serve to bring together the already-committed,

---

[24] This is similar to the Ukrainian tradition, mentioned in chapter three.

and help to keep them committed. In this sense, they are a self-selecting group: only those Catholics who, though totally free (perhaps for the first time) *not* to have anything much to do with religion, nevertheless choose to do so. Szymon, for example, was already a religiously committed teenager when he arrived at university. Childhood altar-serving developed, over time, into a great love for (as he calls it) 'the Sacred Liturgy'. By sixth form, he was his parish's head altar server, heavily involved in training up the younger ones. As one of the few faithful students at his Catholic high school, he had also become deeply interested in apologetics in order to defend the Faith – and himself – to his classmates. He came to university expecting this to continue, leading him to seek out the Catholic Society where he could be part of a community where he could support and be supported. This clearly worked; Szymon is now discerning a vocation with a traditionalist congregation.

Secondly, however, they can also – when they are successful, at least – exert a gravitational pull on others in their orbit to various degrees. These may include non-Catholic friends being attracted through invitations to talks or social events, or else just belonging to a social circle that contains several CathSoc-ers: across the country's universities, a good number of conversions happen this way each year. But they also include less-committed Catholics being brought, perhaps gradually, to see their given religion in a new light. Erin is a good example. Though raised Catholic, she primarily signed up to CathSoc to make new friends.

> I think because I hadn't grown up particularly with a faith, I didn't really understand the importance of things like, why you don't have sex outside of marriage. It was just, 'don't do it'. There was never any actual reason. It was… just this rule that I was told. But actually, there's all… the value in the person and the relationship behind what you're doing and the reasons for it, that I didn't understand then.

As we sat eating our recently delivered Nando's on the carpet of her student hall of residence's floor, Erin recounted how having the supportive environment of CathSoc led her to know that anything could be discussed, even the most personally raw topics. Like Tom above, she appreciated not being judged for the fact that she didn't know certain Church teachings, that no one would think any less of her for asking. This led her to tell me that she had experienced a lot of personal growth in the months since she'd joined CathSoc.

Familiar messages, new methods

Plurality – or competing truth claims – is a fact of life for these students. They are under no illusions that there are other, decidedly non-Catholic ways to view the world. Whilst the 'what' of the Faith may not have changed, the 'how' certainly has.[25] What for previous generations may have been something to take for granted – 'once a Catholic, always a Catholic', etc. – has now become a deliberate choice. Two things in particular strike us about the situation that Catholic students find themselves in. On the one hand, large numbers of participants attribute their current practice and habits to upbringing in the Faith, assuming a cultural continuity to anchor them through the ups and downs of early adulthood. Religion can be as natural and comforting then as a mother tongue. On the other, the students know their beliefs are consciously *other*, and adopt a somewhat detached disposition in order to understand how their 'normal' beliefs are – at best – strange to many they encounter.

In the media, most references to Christian university groups – such as, 'Oxford College student U-turn over Christian Union ban'[26] – have traditionally come about following disputes between

---

[25] Peter, Berger, *The Many Altars of Modernity: Toward a Paradigm for Religion in a Pluralist Age* (New York: De Gruyter, 2014), 32.

[26] BBC News, 'Oxford College student U-turn over Christian Union ban', 10 October 2017, <https://www.bbc.co.uk/news/uk-england-oxfordshire-41565132>.

the (typically very secular) Student Union and the particularly 'zealous' form of Christianity that is conservative evangelicalism.[27] More recently, however, Catholic groups have been increasingly the subject of such headlines in relation to pro-life issues where unequivocal opposition to abortion has troubled the Student Union or students themselves.[28] More broadly, Adam spoke about the hope that the younger, more self-consciously orthodox believers can bring:

> Undoing some of these 1960s experiments will go a long way. I think you could understand at the time when the idea was to open the Church up to the world, and there would be this conversion. 'If we became more like the world, then the world would *like* us, and… the gap between us and the world would [become] narrow[er] so people could jump across and come over to the Catholic side'. We know that that hasn't happened, we know that what has happened has been the precise opposite.

Adam proposed undoing some of these reforms through the widespread re-introduction of church organs and hymns in Liturgy, the priest celebrating Mass *ad orientem*, in the hope of 'reasserting our own identity', which he thought might bring more to the Faith. 'If they see, you know, Catholicism as something which is solid, which is long lasting, and which is firm in its convictions that can

---

[27] Matthew Guest, Sonya Sharma, Kristin Aune, and Rob Warner, 'Challenging "Belief" and the Evangelical Bias: Student Christianity in English Universities', *Journal of Contemporary Religion* 28/2, 207-223, at 208.

[28] E.g., Madoc Cairns, 'Stirling Catholic Student Society Suspended over Abortion Post', *The Tablet*, 7 March 2023, <https://www.thetablet.co.uk/news/16766/stirling-catholic-student-society-suspended-over-abortion-post>. In February 2024, students at University of Manchester organised a change.org petition, campaigning to 'Dissolve the Pro-Life Society at the University of Manchester' which at the time of writing (March 2024) had gained over 19,000 signatures. See petition at: <https://www.change.org/p/dissolve-the-pro-life-society-at-the-university-of-manchester>.

encourage people to join'. When I asked whether he thought that was realistic with his current generation, he explained:

> I think it's the most realistic… because the people in our generation, are so… there's been such a massive attrition, most people are by default so liberal, that only a self-consciously countercultural Catholicism will be able to work and will be able to maintain itself… as a viable political force. And as a force, which, let's face it, above all, the goal of the Church is not to be a bit of an actor, one among many, but, you know, to lead people to the Truth. And I think, to be a lighthouse, you know, to be a lighthouse in the darkness, you need to have your own authentic vision of the world, and you need to proclaim it, unapologetically.

He also seemed to think that Catholicism may have a chance with disillusioned liberals who he believed acquiesced in the status quo:

> There are a lot of young people that I know, that go along because they think it's the only way… they go along because they think this is what they should be doing. A lot of people are not really interested in… flying the Gay Pride flag, a lot of people are not really interested in stuff. They go along because it's there. They go along because they watch *Netflix*, and that's what's there. But if there was a *real* alternative, if there was an unapologetic alternative, they would turn to that, you know, and of course… a good example of that is *this* one.

As a History and War Studies student, we might expect that Adam would be used to adopting the long view towards matters of culture and civilisation. This also appeared to be the results of a series of long-term thought experiments where he observed the logical conclusions of ideas. For him, the current and ideological cultural climate was unstable and illogical. Adam had witnessed the social consequences of contemporary culture's indifference to God and believed that the Faith could be posited as a real alternative to social woes. Listening to Adam, I was struck by the fearlessness with which he discussed these topics. What is more, such views were not particularly uncommon within the CathSoc.

The students' representation of faith on campus is similar to that of the evangelical form: 'discursive, presented in reasonable argument, and foreground[s] cognitive, propositional belief in its expression of Christian identity'.[29] Precisely because of the increasing estrangement of explicitly Christian ideas from the mainstream, the stronger the desire or fervour becomes on the part of the students, who go out of their way, to understand *what* the Faith is, and as a consequence what this means for their daily affairs. Whilst most will not be committing their life to the supernatural vocations of priesthood and religious life, states previously thought of as 'hard core', even the lay vocation now appears to carry the association of 'keen'. Spending evenings listening to religious academics give public lectures on the Letter to the Hebrews, theological responses to the Covid-19 lockdown, or the Church's teaching on animal rights, demonstrated the willingness of the students to claim that the Catholic worldview is able to encompass such a wide variety of topics. This sustains two lungs: the intellectual – opportunities to think, deliberate, and discuss ideas, and the social – in-person encounters with like-minded others, and the active sustaining of these relationships, whether vertically (inter-generationally, as well as academically) or horizontally (among peers). For the students, it was clear that it was not enough to simply affiliate with Catholicism. For the affiliation to have *any* weight or meaning, it had to be personally owned and understood, *especially* if it was meant to be shared with others. They took seriously the notion that the 'keystone' of the European value-system

---

[29] Guest et al., 'Challenging "Belief" and the Evangelical Bias', 208.

is slowly crumbling with few people understanding the religious materials that allowed it to first be erected.[30]

Conclusion

The students in this study mentioned frequently the importance of a space for questions and learning. It let the students know that not only was it okay – praiseworthy, even – to be intellectually curious, but because the questions mattered to the chaplains, mysteriously the students found they mattered to God. Feeling seen and heard in this way, the students find a place for themselves in the institutional Church, several of them in a very direct sense through religious vocations.

Anyone interested in the future of religion has to be interested in the trends exhibited by the youth today. Research in chaplaincies show us that young people are an investment and need to be helped to prepare for the future. Within a generation or two's time, it is these students, and others like them, who will be leading the Church, both in the religious sphere as clergy and religious, and in all manner of lay roles. Pope Francis has stressed since the early years of his pontificate that we are 'not living an era of change but a change of era'.[31] Whilst we cannot predict with any certainty where present trends are leading, we know that Pope Benedict XVI's late-1960s prediction that the Church 'will become small' and 'no longer be able to inhabit many of the edifices she built in prosperity'[32] has already largely come to pass. He goes on: 'the future of the Church, once again as always, will be reshaped by saints... by men [sic], that is, whose minds probe

---

[30] Grace Davie, *Europe, the Exceptional Case: Parameters of Faith in the Modern World* (London: Darton, Longman, and Todd, 2002), 46.

[31] Joshua J. McElwee, 'Catholicism Can and Must Change, Francis Forcefully Tells Italian Church Gathering', 10 November 2015, <https://www.ncronline.org/catholicism-can-and-must-change-francis-forcefully-tells-italian-church-gathering>.

[32] Benedict XVI, *Faith and the Future* (San Francisco, CA: Ignatius Press, 2009), 114.

deeper than the slogans of the day, who see more than others see, because their lives embrace a wider reality'.[33] The voluntarism essential to contemporary young British Catholicism is shaping us up for this new way of being Church.

Chaplaincy is clearly very valuable, primarily because it is meeting students where they are at a critical juncture in their lives. Most of these students fit into the twenty-somethings bracket, meaning that they are in the so-called 'defining decade'. Approximately '80% of life's most defining moments take place by age 35': career choices, who – or whether – to marry, personality changes, and the establishment of social networks.[34] Religious commitment in one's student years is no guarantee of religious commitment later in life. But it is certainly a good predictor. And if one happens to find a religious vocation, or one's also-committed-Catholic life partner, while there, all the better.

Students were well aware that the community experience there is unique. This means that they were less likely to take it for granted, and consequently less likely to forget it. Knowing that they are in a minority, the students have to walk the tightrope of accommodation and avoidance (cutting themselves off from the culture in case of ideological contamination). They represent an increasingly rare category which affirms the desire both to believe in Christ and to belong to His Church. It is precisely because Catholic university students associate themselves with the Faith in this way – believing *and* belonging, willingly – that our attention is warranted.

---

[33] Ibid.

[34] Meg Jay, *The Defining Decade: Why your Twenties Matters and How to Make the Most of Them* (Edinburgh: Canongate Books, 2012), xvi.

5. Latin Massers (and the Liturgical Long Tail)

Back in Preston, a mere half-mile from chapter three's Syro-Malabar Cathedral of St Alphonsa, is another large – 'cavernous, barn-like', according to our scribbled fieldwork notes – nineteenth-century church: St Thomas of Canterbury and the English Martyrs. Designed by Edward Welby Pugin, its foundation stone was laid in 1866, before a crowd of 10,000 local Catholics singing 'Faith of our Fathers'. Even though the original church could fit 700, a decade later the architect was brought back to enlarge it.[1] Fast-forward a further century and a half, thanks to (in the words of the then Bishop of Lancaster) 'a dwindling Mass attendance and a sharp deterioration in its maintenance',[2] the church risked closure.

St Walburge's, itself less than a mile from our other two, is older and larger still. Work began in spring 1850, several months before the Restoration of the Hierarchy, but the idea was always to make a statement. Designed by Joseph Hansom, the church's 309 ft spire – the UK's third or fifth tallest, depending on one's source – still dominates the Preston skyline. Situated in an area of the city that used to consist, but hasn't for a long time, largely of Mass-going millworkers, its more recent history is a now-familiar one. Following a significant

---

1. See archived version of the old parish website: <https://web.archive.org/web/20130503102311/http://www.englishmartyrspreston.org.uk/history1.htm>.
2. Michael Campbell, 'Entrusting the English Martyrs' Church, Preston to the ICKSP', *The Bishop's Blog*, 23 September 2017, <https://bishopswarbricks.blog/2017/09/23/entrusting-the-english-martyrs-church-preston-to-the-icksp/>.

period of under-use, and with growing upkeep costs, the Grade I-listed building was named one of the Victorian Society's Top Ten Endangered Buildings in 2007 in the wake of the diocese's plans to close it.³ Parishioners and local well-wishers rallied in the only way that Lancastrians know how hot pot suppers, raffles, and real ale festivals. Nevertheless, the future looked bleak.

Fortunately, help was at hand from what has become a common salve to British bishops' headaches: a religious congregation from Africa.⁴ The Institute of Christ the King Sovereign Priest (ICKSP), founded in Gabon in 1990, is one of a small number of religious congregations devoted to the Extraordinary Form – or Traditional Latin Mass (TLM), *usus antiquior*, old rite – that is, to the expression of the Roman liturgy in use prior to the changes enacted following the Second Vatican Council.⁵ St Walburge's was entrusted to the ICKSP as a shrine church in 2014; English Martyrs was added in 2017.

The work to be done at both sites was, and still is, an uphill battle. After all, if the basic reasons why they were creatively redeployed in the first place – low attendance, overstretched clergy, ruinous renovation costs – were easily solvable, they'd probably still be ordinary parishes. But things look promising. In the first place, they have a scarce chunk of ecclesial capital: human resources. The Preston mission has two priests for the two churches. In 2018, they were joined by a small community of religious sisters, the Sisters Adorers of the Royal Heart of Jesus Sovereign Priest (i.e., the ICKSP's

---

3 'Funds Push for Threatened Historic Preston Church', *Lancashire Telegraph*, 22 August 2008, <https://www.lancashiretelegraph.co.uk/news/3616129.funds-push-threatened-historic-preston-church/>.

4 For example, the nearby Marian shrine of Ladyewell (a whole three miles away from St Alphonsa's, St Walburge's, and English Martyrs was entrusted in 2015 to the Institute of the Holy Family Fathers and Brothers of the Youth, founded in Nigeria in 2002. See Conor Gaffey, 'Lancaster Shrine Saved by Nigerian Religious Order', *Catholic Herald*, 9 February 2015, https://catholicherald.co.uk/lancaster-shrine-saved-by-nigerian-religious-order/.

5 Shaun Blanchard and Stephen Bullivant, *Vatican II: A Very Short Introduction* (Oxford: Oxford University Press, 2023), 37–51.

female branch). They live in the former presbytery of yet another large nineteenth-century church, St Augustine's, which closed in the 1980s. It, too, is within a mile of the others.[6] 'The Spire and the Martyrs', as the Institute's quasi-parish brands itself, thus has a much higher 'staffing ratio' than many churches in the area.

In the second place, by both offering something distinctive and doing it well, St Walburge's and English Martyrs attract a gathered community that transcends the old parish boundaries. While the Extraordinary Form might be the preferred Mass of only a small percentage in any one parish, it is sufficiently attractive for those people – some of them all the time, some part of the time – to travel in from the surrounding area, and to feel sufficiently invested that they work towards building up and sustaining the community, and therefore its buildings, for the future.

A Sunday morning visit to St Walburge's makes clear its work-in-progress nature – with emphases on both *work* and *progress*. The church's grimy exterior, testament to Preston's industrial past, has significant portions covered in scaffolding. Inside is a remarkable study in contrasts: blackened walls, peeling paintwork, buckets carefully positioned thanks to a leaking roof. But these serve starkly to emphasise the lovingly up-kept carpentry, marblework, and embroidery, richly adorning the things that matter most: the sanctuary, side altars, memorials, saints. The latter are a particular feature. I counted around fifty full-size statues, filling every available plinth or other space. The overall impression was of a sanctuary for discarded saints: refugees from church closures spared from eBay or a skip, carefully restored and – more to the point – *used* for

---

[6] This is a point worth stressing. Within a mile radius of St Alphonsa's are not only St Walburge's, English Martyrs, and the (defunct) St Augustine's, but three other (open) churches: St Wilfrid's, St Joseph's, and St Gregory the Great. Another church, St Teresa's, closed for worship in 2011. Extending the radius an extra mile adds perhaps another seven currently operating Catholic churches. The sheer density of churches means that Preston's present worshipping community is thinned out over an infrastructure built for many times more people. So too, of course, are the clergy.

devotional purposes. And while the huge nave is a long way from full, there's a decent-sized congregation: skewing younger, and with a higher proportion of children and men, than one typically finds in the area. Furthermore, it's clear from browsing the bulletins and noticeboard that this is an actively engaged community: quiz nights, family catechesis, guilds, a co-op for homeschooling families, prolife activities, pilgrimages, classes for 'catechumens and neophytes', fundraising for both renovations and seminarians, and – naturally – hot pot suppers to celebrate saints' days.

Preston provides a particularly good example of both present pastoral realities, especially in Britain's erstwhile Catholic heartlands, and some of the creative responses that several dioceses have been making in light of them. But it is far from the only one. In the north west alone, the ICKSP has care of the iconic 'Dome from Home' (i.e., SS Peter and Paul, and St Philomena) in New Brighton, Merseyside. Another traditionalist congregation, the Priestly Fraternity of St Peter (FSSP) runs St Mary's in the centre of Warrington. Both groups are present elsewhere in the country too, whether in semi-permanent shrine churches or personal parishes, or with regular 'borrowed space' in existing parishes.[7] Very similar stories could be told about most or all of these places: surplus or underused churches; religious orders with ready and willing clergy; and a motivated laity drawn from a reasonably wide catchment area, some of whom attend every week (or day), and others who make the trip less often while remaining committed members of their home parishes too. In this regard, Latin Mass[8] congregations are very similar to the various 'diasporic'

---

[7] A small number of other congregations, dedicated partly or fully to the Latin Mass, are also present in Britain. These include the Marian Franciscans (Portsmouth and Dundee), the Sons of the Most Holy Redeemer (Papa Stronsay, Orkneys), and the Franciscan Sisters of the Immaculate (Lanherne, Cornwall).

[8] 'Latin Mass' is a common shorthand, and will be used extensively here, to refer to the Extraordinary Form or Traditional Latin Mass. It is worth remembering, however, that Vatican II required no wholesale de-Latinization as part of the liturgical reforms. The Novus Ordo is celebrated in its original Latin in some British churches too.

congregations highlighted in chapter three, with the exception that the former are much more likely to mirror the overall demographics of an area's Catholic population.[9]

As with most subgroups in the Church, it is difficult to estimate the size of the Latin Mass community nationwide – or even to know quite *who* one actually means. There is no very clear or meaningful distinction to be drawn (as one sometimes sees done) between 'Extraordinary Form Catholics' and 'Novus Ordo Catholics'. Very few Latin Massers have both the inclination and luxury to attend Latin Masses exclusively. And many of those in any given Sunday TLM congregation will also be regular attendees of (non-TLM) Masses, whether in the same church or in other parishes. No doubt there is a small percentage in many parishes who would, all other things being equal, prefer to attend a Latin Mass as their regular Sunday Mass. But other things are rarely equal. Someone who would opt for a Latin Mass in their own parish, if available, might still not be willing to drive an extra twenty minutes to a neighbouring parish every week for one. Someone else might routinely trek an hour or more every week, with young kids in the car.

More concretely, on any given Sunday, there are maybe 3-4,000 Britons attending Mass in the Extraordinary Form.[10] The vast majority of those will have had to 'travel in' to some extent.

---

[9] See Joseph Shaw, 'The Traditional Latin Mass and Diversity', in *The Liturgy, The Family and the Crisis of Modernity: Essays of a Traditional Catholic* (Lincoln, NE: Os Justi Press, 2023), 148–56.

[10] A *very* rough estimate. It is based on recent, confirmed Mass counts of: the Brompton Oratory (200), ICKSP Preston (200), FSSP (1,000 across Britain and Ireland, but with only one site in the latter, so c. 900 as a conservative figure for just Britain). Scotland as a whole had c. 450 at Sunday TLMs in 2019, though overall provision has reduced in recent years (see below); so call it 400 at the top end. So that's c. 1,700 so far. All that accounts for only about a quarter of the British TLMs happening each Sunday, albeit with a skew towards some of the better attended ones. A good number of the remainder, we suspect, will have congregations in the low two-digits. So doubling the number seems reasonable-ish: 3,400.

Thanks to Fr Uwe Michael Lang Cong. Orat., Fr Armand de Malleray FSSP, and Michael Durnan for their statistics. Scottish figures for 2019 taken from Una Voce Scotland, 'FIUV Annual Survey', *Holy Cross* (newsletter), March 2020, 10.

To be clear: the congregation at St Mary's, Warrington, is a thoroughly local one. But even so, very few will live in the centre of Warrington itself. Likewise, St Walburge's regulars are mostly drawn from the 'Greater Preston' area, including various villages and small towns such as Leyland, Penwortham, and Longridge. Others come from as far afield as Lancaster, including a small contingent of university students. Of course, for reasons detailed in chapter one, that is true for a lot of thriving parishes, 'Trad' or not. It is also true of the diasporic and/or Eastern Catholic congregations in chapter three. That in itself is a good reason for thinking that TLM-attending Catholics will be more religiously committed in terms of the 'three Bs' of believing, behaving, and belonging even than the average Mass-going Catholic.[11] Even going to Mass at all these days is a strong indicator of commitment; to be willing to travel (much) further than necessary marks one out as someone who really cares.[12] It may well be that Latin Massers tend to be *more* committed/orthodox/pious even than other niche groups. We could well believe it, though the research has yet to be done.

From Summorum Pontificum...

In July 2007, Pope Benedict XVI promulgated the apostolic letter *Summorum Pontificum*. This recognised that, notwithstanding the significant liturgical changes undertaken during and after the Second Vatican Council, 'in some regions… not a few of the faithful continued to be attached with such love and affection to the earlier liturgical forms which had deeply shaped their culture

---

[11] On the 'three Bs', see Ben Clements and Stephen Bullivant, *Catholics in Contemporary Britain: Faith, Society, Politics* (Oxford: Oxford University Press, 2022), 32–92.

[12] Let us not be misunderstood. Lots of highly committed Catholics go to their nearest parish church too. But only the relatively highly committed are willing to travel further than necessary. So any church, whatever its liturgical offering, that attracts higher-than-average numbers of 'commuters', will *ipso facto* have a higher-than-average number of the highly committed.

and spirit'.¹³ Over the years, Rome had authorised a number of pastoral accommodations for such people. These began with a 1971 'indult' from Pope St Paul VI, following Cardinal Heenan's presentation of a petition organised by the Latin Mass Society (founded in April 1965):

> 'Considering the pastoral needs referred to by Your Eminence, it is permitted to the local Ordinaries of England and Wales to grant that certain groups of the faithful may on special occasions be allowed to participate in the Mass celebrated according to the Rites and texts of the former Roman Missal...'¹⁴

This local permission was universalised by Pope St John Paul II in 1984's *Quattuor Abhinc Annos*, and reiterated in 1988's *Ecclesia Dei* with the request that 'respect must everywhere by shown for the feelings of all those who are attached to the Latin liturgical tradition by a wide and generous application'.¹⁵ Pope Benedict's new document, however, constituted a significant liberalisation of what it now termed the 'extraordinary form of the Church's liturgy'. Replacing the previous requirement for special permissions being granted by a bishop (who then had to submit annual reports to

---

13 Benedict XVI, *Summorum Pontificum* (2007), <https://www.vatican.va/content/benedict-xvi/en/motu_proprio/documents/hf_ben-xvi_motu-proprio_20070707_summorum-pontificum.html>.

14 Text available at: <https://lms.org.uk/heenan-indult>. On the wider context, see Joseph Shaw (ed.), *The Latin Mass and the Intellectuals: Petitions to the Save the Ancient Mass from 1966 to 2007* (Waterloo: Arouca Press, 2023); and Alcuin Reid (ed.), *A Bitter Trial: Evelyn Waugh and John Cardinal Heenan on the Liturgical Changes*, rev. edn (San Francisco, CA: Ignatius Press, 2011). For an interesting perspective on grassroots traditionalism, see Brandon Reece Taylorian, 'The Struggle of Traditionalist Catholics in 1970s Northern England', *North West Catholic History* 50/1 (2023), 45–65.

15 Congregation for Divine Worship, *Quattuor Abhinc Annos* (1988), <https://www.vatican.va/roman_curia/pontifical_commissions/ecclsdei/documents/hf_jp-ii_motu-proprio_02071988_ecclesia-dei_en.html https://lms.org.uk/quattuor-abhinc-annos>; John Paul II, *Ecclesia Dei* (1988), <https://www.vatican.va/roman_curia/pontifical_commissions/ecclsdei/documents/hf_jp-ii_motu-proprio_02071988_ecclesia-dei_en.html>.

Rome on what permissions had been granted to whom), *Summorum Pontificum* essentially devolved these decisions to individual priests. Furthermore, 'where a group of the faithful attached to the previous liturgical tradition stably exists', parish priests are urged 'willingly [to] accede to their requests' for these liturgies. Critically, he should also 'ensure that the good of these members of the faithful is harmonised with the ordinary pastoral care of the parish'.

Benedict XVI's intention, clearly, was for a normalisation of the Extraordinary Form, *and moreover its adherents*, within the usual pastoral life of the Church. Over four decades on from the Council, the old Mass remained spiritually important for a committed minority of both clergy and laypeople, many of whom had not been raised with it. What is more, for the vast majority of these, this devotion was in no way part of an oppositional attitude to the wider Church, or the Second Vatican Council, or to any other valid liturgical options.[16] Since their absolute numbers are not huge, there is no risk of whole swathes of the Church suddenly 'going Trad' – as Benedict XVI happily acknowledged: 'The use of the old Missal presupposes a certain degree of liturgical formation and some knowledge of the Latin language; neither of these is found very often.... [I]t is clearly seen that the new Missal will certainly remain the ordinary Form of the Roman Rite, not only on account of the juridical norms, but also because of the actual situation of the communities of the faithful.'[17]

---

[16] Such people and communities do exist in the wider traditionalist movement, including in a number of schismatic or otherwise canonically irregular groups (reconciling some of whom was also clearly one of Benedict's hopes), but a love for the older liturgical form can, and for the very most part does, exist apart from all that. Indeed, this had always been the case: 'Many people who clearly accepted the binding character of the Second Vatican Council, and were faithful to the Pope and the Bishops, nonetheless also desired to recover the form of the sacred liturgy that had been dear to them.' (Joseph Shaw, 'The Crisis of the 1960s', in Shaw (ed.), *Latin Mass and the Intellectuals*, loc. 2071.)

[17] Benedict XVI, 'Letter to the Bishops on the Occasion of the Publication of the Apostolic Letter "*motu proprio data*" Summorum Pontificum on the Use of the Roman Liturgy Prior to the Reform of 1970', https://www.vatican.va/content/benedict-xvi/en/letters/2007/documents/hf_ben-xvi_let_20070707_lettera-vescovi.html

Summorum Pontificum does specifically allow for dioceses to create 'personal parishes' for Latin Mass-preferring Catholics, such as can be used for the special pastoral care of Eastern Catholics (remembering, as noted in chapter three, that St Alphonsa's was originally erected as such for Preston's Syro-Malabars), specific national or language groups, or other specific groupings (some US dioceses have, for example, dedicated African-American, Charismatic, or Social Justice parishes). However, the general expectation of the document seems to be that it will mostly apply to ordinary parishes and priests offering the Extraordinary Form as part of the usual menu of liturgical offerings.

After *Summorum Pontificum*, there were two main developments, both of which happened slowly and in a piecemeal fashion. The most obvious one was precisely the kind of thing we've seen already: some bishops, in some dioceses, creating (semi-)permanent homes for the Extraordinary Form in particular areas. As noted, dedicated religious congregations have been the go-to guys for these initiatives. Strictly speaking, this is not necessary. It is perfectly possible for a bishop to create a personal parish for TLM devotees, and to staff it with his own suitably trained clergy; elsewhere, this has indeed been done.[18] However, as is clear from our Preston case study, designating certain churches for Latin Massers (or Syro-Malabars, for that matter) has allowed bishops to solve several other problems as well. One can *both* genuinely care for the pastoral good of the Trads in your flock, *and* be relieved to free up short-supply clergy for other duties, get a seven-figure repair bill for a listed building off your desk, generate some welcome 'historic church saved!' PR in the local press, plus see some energetic missionary priests and sisters deployed to some of the country's grittier neo-evangelistic mission fields.

---

[18] For example, the Archdiocese of Melbourne, Australia.

The other, more subtle fruit was precisely the primary one hoped for by *Summorum Pontificum*. Gradually, the Extraordinary Form became a normal-if-a-bit-niche part of otherwise ordinary parishes up and down the country. More priests, especially younger ones, learned how to celebrate it, both for their own spiritual interest and edification, and to be able 'willingly [to] accede' to the requests of current or future laity. The odd Extraordinary Form became, if not exactly common, then at least no longer scarce on parish timetables. Very rarely, if ever, did these displace any of the existing parish Sunday services. Instead, a priest might replace one of his weekday or Saturday morning Masses with an EF, or else add in an extra weekly or monthly Mass, either in the early morning or the afternoon. These would typically attract a certain proportion of local parishioners, but also a semi-regular clientele drawn from a wider area. In some places, especially big-city churches served by a congregation such as the Oratorians or the Dominicans,[19] a regular Sunday Mass might consistently attract a congregation of a hundred or two. But elsewhere – at the weekly 12pm at a tiny, pre-Restoration of the Hierarchy church in an Oxfordshire hamlet, say, or at the monthly 3pm in a 1960s Nottingham church on what was once Europe's biggest council estate[20] – numbers might be much lower. It could be twelve one week, thirty the next, depending largely on the presence or not of one or two large families. Depending on where you lived, you could be relatively spoilt for choice, or else a three-hour round trip away (or much farther in rural areas, especially in Scotland). And as we've seen

---

[19] These are not, of course, traditionalist congregations like the FSSP or ICKSP. However, over the years (and long predating *Summorum Pontificum*) both have had a sufficient number of able and willing priests to have consistently offered either the Extraordinary Form or the (closely related) Dominican Rite in some of their churches. The Oratories, especially, are known for this, and probably attract the largest regular EF congregations in the country.

[20] Both real examples: Holy Trinity, Hethe, and Corpus Christi, Clifton.

with many foreign-language Masses, provision might suddenly stop when a particular priest retired or relocated.

Nevertheless, when we started the fieldwork for this project, it was already clear that the Latin Mass world had been slowly growing over the past decade or so since *Summorum Pontificum*. On the eve of the pandemic, an average of 57 Latin Masses were held each Sunday in England and Wales.[21] They were held in every diocese bar one (Hallam), with particular hotspots including Portsmouth (averaging eight each Sunday), Liverpool, Birmingham, and Southwark (all averaging five). In Scotland, there were nine Masses on a typical Sunday, with diocesan highs in Glasgow and Aberdeen (three each, albeit with two of Aberdeen's happening in the Orkneys).[22] Several bishops, moreover, could occasionally be seen celebrating in the Extraordinary Form, for example on visitations of parishes with regular Masses, or when conducting Confirmations and Ordinations for the traditionalist congregations. There was also, as there still is, a regular calendar of regional or national Masses and pilgrimages – Carfin, Walsingham, Oxford – organised by the Latin Mass Society or Una Voce Scotland.

All in all, the post-*Summorum Pontificum* situation is well-summarised by the Latin Mass Society's chairman, Dr Joseph Shaw:

> [A]s the years passed there were more and more places in which the bishop's diminishing aversion to it ceased to outweigh increasing demands from priests and people. It helped that there were more and more priests available to celebrate it, whether from the Traditional Priestly Institutes or the younger generation of diocesan priests, and, in the context of the accelerating decline of the Church in the developed world, an ever-increasing number of redundant church buildings.

---

[21] We are grateful to the Latin Mass Society for these and other figures.
[22] Una Voce Scotland, 'Traditional Mass in Scotland', *Holy Cross* (newsletter), March 2020, 11–12.

This meant that by negotiation, experimentation, and taking the opportunities of manpower and real estate which presented themselves in the course of time, establishing or allowing celebrations of the Old Mass solved problems for the bishops: what to do with an historic church, how to get a group of Traditional Catholics off his back, how to satisfy the desires of certain priests. Once that had happened, bishops would often begin to appreciate the fruits of the apostolates which emerged: the marriages and baptisms, the feeling of being treated like a real old-fashioned bishop when visiting the parish, the outsized financial contributions, and above all the vocations, many of them coming into the diocesan seminary.[23]

...*to* Traditionis Custodes

In July 2021, fourteen years after Benedict's, Pope Francis promulgated a new apostolic letter 'on the use of the Roman liturgy prior to the Reform of 1970'. This came following 'a detailed consultation of the [world's] bishops', co-ordinated by the Congregation for the Doctrine of the Faith. *Traditionis Custodes*, as the document was called, not only repealed a good deal of the prior document's permissions, but added several brand-new restrictions to celebrations (and indeed celebrants) of the Traditional Latin Mass. Gone is the talk of there being two cherished 'Forms' of the Roman rite, Ordinary and Extraordinary. Instead, 'The liturgical books promulgated by St Paul VI and St John Paul II, in conformity with the decrees of Vatican Council II, are the unique [*unica*] expression of the *lex orandi* of the Roman

---

[23] Joseph Shaw, 'Is the Missal of Paul VI the *Unum Necessarium*?', in Peter A. Kwasniewski (ed.), *From Benedict's Peace to Francis' War: Catholics Respond to the* Motu Proprio Traditionis Custodes *on the Latin Mass* (Brooklyn, NY: Angelico Press, 2021), 374–401, at 398. Dr Shaw has been hugely helpful in informing several aspects of this chapter, as also has Revd Dr Stephen Morgan.

Rite'.[24] 'Unique' here appears to mean 'special' or 'pre-eminent', rather than 'only', however, since celebrations 'according to the Missal antecedent to the reform of 1970' remain valid and permitted,[25] albeit under much heavier constraints.

Henceforth, bishops should 'designate one or more locations where the faithful adherents of these [already existing] groups may gather for the eucharistic celebration'. Yet these are *not* to be 'parochial churches', nor are any new personal parishes allowed to be created.[26] They must also 'take care not to authorise the establishment of new groups'.[27] Priests who already celebrate these Masses must obtain permission from their bishop to continue. Any newly ordained priests who wish to start must seek permission from their bishop, who must then consult Rome before granting it.

In the week or so following *Traditionis Custodes*, I[28] found myself at Holy Rood, Oxford, on a Sunday evening. The Latin Mass here had started a few years before, after clergy moves had 'orphaned' an existing local group. Holy Rood's resident priest, a member of the Ordinariate, had generously offered to accommodate them, despite numbers never being massive. (Oxford also has another, much larger Latin Mass group, with a regular early-morning Mass at the Oratory.) 'I think we're quite nice, actually', was one mother's hurt reaction to the new directives. Otherwise, it was business as usual, at least for the time being. Few bishops, at this early stage, had decided how to go about implementing the new norms, or indeed quite how 'normative' some of them actually were. There was hope, at least in some quarters, that the text's stringent regulations were

---

[24] Francis, *Traditionis Custodes* (2001), available online at: *https://www.vatican.va/content/francesco/en/motu_proprio/documents/20210716-motu-proprio-traditionis-custodes.html*.

[25] We leave aside here, as does the document itself, the precise status of various other forms of the Roman rite, such as the Ordinariate's Divine Worship (whose liturgical books were promulgated not by St Paul VI or St John Paul II, but by Benedict XVI).

[26] *Traditionis Custodes*, art. 3, §2.

[27] Ibid., art. 3, §6.

[28] I.e., SB.

really intended to empower bishops to deal decisively with certain 'problem' congregations, when and where needed, while for the most part going unenforced elsewhere on legitimate pastoral grounds. Why else, on this line of thinking, would the text be at pains to stress that 'it belongs to the diocesan bishop, as moderator, promoter, and guardian of the whole liturgical life of the particular Church entrusted to him, to regulate the liturgical celebrations of his diocese', and affirm that it his 'exclusive competence to authorise the use of the 1962 Roman Missal' there? Problems might exist elsewhere, but not obviously in Britain. Indeed, one senior bishop was heard to comment that since Latin Masses were celebrated by some of his best priests, and were one of the few places in his diocese attracting young men, he had little desire to change the *status quo*. Evidently, his sentiments were quite widely shared. In only a few dioceses were Latin Masses significantly reduced, or in one place stopped, more or less immediately. Overall, they continued their pre-Covid, pre-*Traditionis Custodes* modest growth curve. A year on, in Summer 2022, there were 70 each Sunday in Britain, up from 66 in 2019.

Yet as time went on, the original rules were clarified and/or tightened in response to queries or attempted work-arounds. For example, in the case of new priests seeking permission to celebrate, it was made clear that *Traditionis Custodes*' 'consult' really means 'request permission from' Rome. Most notably here, it was conceded that, if nowhere else suitable is available, parish churches *could* be used (though only with Rome's express say-so). Nonetheless, it is stressed that the general rule 'is intended to affirm that the celebration of the Eucharist according to the previous rite, being a concession limited to these groups, is not part of the ordinary life of the parish community'. Hence, when and where parish churches *are* permitted to be used, 'such a celebration should not be included in the parish Mass schedule', and 'it should not be held at the same time as the pastoral activities of the parish community.'

Lest it somehow be thought otherwise, readers are assured that: 'There is no intention in these provisions to marginalise the faithful who are rooted in the previous form of celebration'.[29]

As time has gone on, various concrete effects of *Traditionis Custodes* have started to be seen. Certainly, there have been a growing number of refusals and restrictions in various places. In some places, the overall detriment is very clear. Just a few months before the release of *Traditionis Custodes*, the Archdiocese of Glasgow had just started its fifth weekly Sunday TLM. Three years later, there is now just one. Immaculate Heart of Mary, Balornock, which used to celebrate it six days a week (and twice on Sundays), now has none.[30]

Elsewhere, the picture is a little more open to interpretation. Most notably, 2024 was the first year since the 1990s without a publicly celebrated TLM Triduum in Westminster, and the Cathedral's high altar can no longer be used for the Latin Mass, as it had been twice-a-year since the 1970s. Such moves have been justified as being 'for the sake of the wider provision'.[31] The implication here seems to be that, in order to secure the requisite allowances from Rome, bishops need to prove their *bona fides* regarding the spirit of the new rules in other areas. At present, Westminster's Trads have a number of Latin Mass options (including a monthly low Mass in one of the Cathedral's side chapels). Especially considering that it isn't one of the dioceses with a resident traditionalist community, Westminster is among the country's better-served places. In this

---

[29] Congregation for Divine Worship, '*Responsa ad dubia* on Certain Provisions of the Apostolic Letter *Traditionis Custodes*' (2021), available online: <https://www.vatican.va/roman_curia/congregations/ccdds/documents/rc_con_ccdds_doc_20211204_responsa-ad-dubia-tradizionis-custodes_en.html>.

[30] Craig Williams, 'An Absolute Disgrace': Decision to Cancel Catholic Mass Sparks Fury', *Glasgow Times*, 2 May 2023, <https://www.glasgowtimes.co.uk/news/23496143.an-absolute-disgrace-decision-cancel-catholic-mass-sparks-fury/>.

[31] Thomas Colsy, 'Diocese of Westminster Rescinds 25-year-old Tradition of Celebrating Easter Triduum in the Old Rite', *Catholic Herald*, 28 February 2024, <https://catholicherald.co.uk/diocese-of-westminster-ends-25-year-old-tradition-of-celebrating-easter-triduum-in-the-old-rite/>.

sense, paradoxically perhaps, a couple of high-profile shut-downs – the more high-profile the better, in some respects – might be exactly what is required to allow all this to continue.

Elsewhere still, things seem to be ticking along, if in a deliberately low key way. (To be fair, it is probably easier to do that outside of major metropolitan sees.) Significantly, the main traditionalist orders are exempted from the clergy-directed restrictions of *Traditionis Custodes*, and religious congregations in general tend to have more independence anyway. Furthermore, while ordinary parish churches are problematic, the new rules make no mention of 'shrine churches'. This is a special category of church in canon law, and is especially suitable for historic churches, which can plausibly be designated as diocesan places of pilgrimage. Helpfully, 'Certain privileges can be granted to shrines whenever local circumstances, the large number of pilgrims, and especially the good of the faithful seem to suggest it.'[32] In several dioceses, as we have seen, the main TLM hubs – including those in Preston, Warrington, and New Brighton – were originally set up as 'shrines', and served by such congregations. It is also worth noting that, thank to parish mergers in many dioceses, there are growing numbers of churches that, while remaining an active part of a bigger parish grouping, are not designated as *the* parish church. Such churches, which are still ordinary diocesan ones, can be assigned to host Latin Masses much more easily. In the present climate, these are likely to prove increasingly useful *modi operandi* for well-disposed bishops.

Given everything, it is not surprising if *Summorum Pontificum*'s 'not a few of the faithful [who continue] to be attached with such love and affection to the earlier liturgical forms' should have been made to feel 'distinctly unwelcome'.[33] It does not, however, seem to have deterred

---

[32] *Code of Canon Law*, 1233.

[33] Joseph Shaw, quoted in Luke Coppen, '*Traditionis Custodes* – 1 year on', The Pillar, 15 July 2022, <https://www.pillarcatholic.com/p/traditionis-custodes-1-year-on>.

them from going; if anything, human psychology being what it is, it is likely to have increased their attachment. In those places where the Latin Mass has (so far) gone unscathed, average numbers are reportedly stable or slightly growing. Given that overall Mass attendance in Britain has fallen by 29% since 2019, that in itself is impressive.

The Liturgical Long Tail[34]

As has been noted several times, there are important commonalities to be drawn between Latin Mass and 'diasporic' Eastern Catholic, ethnic, and/or linguistic congregations, as discussed in chapter three. There are also analogies to be drawn between these and many of the parishes showcased in chapter one, and indeed with the university-centred worshipping communities of chapter four. Other groups too – former Anglicans fortunate to be close to a regular Divine Worship liturgy, for instance[35] – would also count here. In essence, all of these are offering something distinctive, with particular appeal to a specific group or groups of Britain's Catholics. To use the economic terminology deployed in chapter one, there is a sense in which they are all offering the same basic 'product' – i.e., sacramental grace, among much else – but packaged and customised to suit different 'market segments'.

While the metaphor here may be off-putting to some, the basic idea is in no sense a controversial one. 'Uniformity in liturgy throughout the Church has never been a Catholic ideal'.[36]

---

[34] This section and the following one has been adapted from Stephen Bullivant, 'Mass Markets and the "Liturgical Long Tail"', *Antiphon* 26/1 (2022), 1–25.

[35] These could easily have constituted a chapter of their own in this book. They didn't, largely because ex-Anglican clergy as a whole are the subject of a separate, forthcoming publication of SB's, and there would have been too much overlap of material between the two.

[36] Adrian Fortescue, *The Mass: A Study of the Roman Liturgy* (London: Longmans, Green, and Co., 1922), 208. See also Fœderatio Internationalis Una Voce, 'Liturgical Pluralism', in Joseph Shaw (ed.), *The Case for Liturgical Restoration: Una Voce Studies on the Traditional Latin Mass* (Brooklyn, NY: Angelico Press, 2019), 19–23.

This is true, most obviously, with the multiplicity of liturgical rites cherished across the twenty-four 'particular churches' which make up the one Catholic Church, only a few of which we have been able to treat in any detail in these pages. But even within the western, Latin Church, there is a plurality of 'rites', 'forms', and 'uses'. The Roman rite alone, 'unique expression' notwithstanding, currently admits of two main variants, Ordinary and Extraordinary (to use the recent, if now seemingly obsolete, terminology), with the former alone having a number of sub-variants or 'uses'. What is more, the Second Vatican Council is very clear on the potential benefits of further customisation. As one of us has argued at length elsewhere,[37] while Vatican II certainly does set forth a specific (and what would these days count as fairly 'conservative') liturgical vision, it permits almost limitless deviations from this norm – i.e., 'legitimate variations and adaptations to different groups, regions, and peoples'[38] – if (and only if) there are strong pastoral reasons for doing so. Indeed, this follows from the logic of the liturgical reform's stated aims: i.e., 'that the sacrifice of the Mass, even in the ritual forms of its celebration, may become pastorally efficacious *to the fullest degree*', 'full and active participation by all the people is the aim to be considered *before all else*'.[39] Obviously, the Catholic Church carefully lays down liturgical rules and parameters,[40]

---

[37] Stephen Bullivant, "'Especially in Mission Territories': New Evangelization and Liturgical (Reform of the) Reform", in *Authentic Liturgical Renewal in Contemporary Perspective*, ed. Uwe Michael Lang (London: T. & T. Clark, 2017), 97–107; Stephen Bullivant, *Mass Exodus: Catholic Disaffiliation in Britain and America since Vatican II* (Oxford: Oxford University Press, 2019), 137–147; Blanchard and Bullivant, Vatican II, 37–51.

[38] *Sacrosanctum Concilium*, § 38, <https://www.vatican.va/archive/hist_councils/ii_vatican_council/documents/vat-ii_const_19631204_sacrosanctum-concilium_en.html>.

[39] Ibid., §§ 49, 14 (emphases added.),

[40] Cf. 'The *ars celebrandi* cannot be reduced to only a rubrical mechanism, much less should it be thought of as imaginative — sometimes wild — creativity without rules. The rite is in itself a norm, and the norm is never an end in itself, but it is always at the service of a higher reality that it means to protect.' (Francis, *Desiderio Desideravi* [2021], § 48, <https://www.vatican.va/content/francesco/en/apost_letters/documents/20220629-lettera-ap-desiderio-desideravi.html>.)

but within these, it admits a great deal of scope for 'legitimate variations and adaptations', if they are *actually* justified in terms of pastoral and evangelistic 'results'. (That 'actually' is worth stressing. *Sacrosanctum Concilium* in fact holds itself to very exacting standards in terms of – to revert here to our business analogy – the reform's Key Performance Indicators.)

In practice, this much is evident in pretty much any parish, at least in a small way. Different Masses are, at least implicitly, intended for different broad constituencies: different life situations (e.g., a Vigil for those working, or attending children's sports, on Sundays; a 'family Mass' that's a bit shorter, with a children's liturgy for the younger ones), different liturgical (high or low) or musical (organ and hymns, plainchant, folk group, none) preferences, etc. Whether the actual Masses offered are indeed 'pastorally efficacious to the fullest degree' for anyone, let alone most worshippers, is a separate question. And to be fair, you can't please everyone all the time. But the basic idea of 'different liturgical strokes, for different Catholic folks' ought to be a familiar one.

But what of some of the smaller, more 'niche' liturgical offerings – and, more to the point, those who desire them? This is where things get a bit more controverted. Evidently, there are people whose 'full and active participation' would be *much better* fostered with either a particular (licit) way of configuring the Novus Ordo by language or some other consideration (e.g., musical), or else with a different Form or Use, or an Eastern rite (e.g., Ukrainian Catholic, Syro-Malabar, etc.). The reasons why these people would find such a Mass more 'pastorally efficacious' could well be very wide ranging, of course, but that need not detain us here. Most of the time, those desiring or requiring[41] a given

---

[41] Strictly speaking, one could argue that Eastern Catholics, particularly, require liturgical options in their 'home' tradition, even if, in practice, that is often not possible or practical. Our point is a bigger one.

Mass are not numerous in any one parish (though obviously, a parish with a high proportion of Spanish speakers might well, and rightly, offer a Spanish language as part of its own regular Sunday menu), over the local area, there are indeed enough such people, willing to travel, to create a sufficiently viable, stable, regular congregation.

This is, in essence, what we mean by the 'liturgical long tail'.[42] That is to say, while most Catholics are happy (enough) with the usual parish fare – and I stress here such terms as 'usual', 'normal', and 'ordinary' are meant as descriptions of their frequency and embeddedness within the mainstream of parish and diocesan liturgical planning, and not as value-judgements (cf. Ordinary Form, Ordinary Time, *Liber usualis*!) – there is in fact a very large range of other possibilities which, all other things being equal, would be preferable for minorities of varying size.

Why we call this a 'long tail' should hopefully be clear by the accompanying graph. It shows the type of Mass weekly churchgoers say they 'most frequently' attend, using data from the recent 'Catholics in Britain' survey fielded in late 2019.[43] The specific breakdowns aren't so important here (the smaller bars, especially, should be regarded as having a significant margin of error) so much as the overall shape of the graph. That is to say, a heavy skew to the left hand side, with three-quarters of weekly Mass-goers attending

---

[42] On this topic in the business and technology literature (wherefrom I'm borrowing it with 'legitimate variations and adaptations'), see especially Chris Anderson, *The Long Tail: Why the Future of Business is Selling Less of More* (New York: Hyperion, 2006); Erik Brynjolfsson, Yu Jeffrey Hu, and Michael D. Smith, 'From Niches to Riches: Anatomy of the Long Tail', *Sloan Management Review* 47, no. 4 (2006), 67-71; and Seth Godin, *We Are All Weird: The Rise of Tribes and the End of Normal* (London: Penguin, 2015).

[43] Further information, data, and analyses can be found in Ben Clements and Stephen Bullivant, *Catholics in Contemporary Britain: Faith, Society, Politics* (Oxford: Oxford University Press, 2022); and Ben Clements and Stephen Bullivant, 'To Conscience First, and to the Pope (Long) Afterwards? British Catholics and their Attitudes towards Morality and Structural Issues Concerning the Catholic Church', *Review of Religious Research* (2021).

an English-language Novus Ordo in their own parish church, and a further one-in-ten attending similar, but travelling somewhere other than their own parish. Obviously, as discussed above, there will be a good deal of 'legitimate variation and adaptation', even within this subset.

But what about the other fifth of Mass-goers? Note figure 1's 'long tail' of minority liturgical preferences which, strictly speaking, could really be extended out into a vastly longer and thinner tail of more specific options. For example, we are grouping all 'foreign language' Masses here into a single category. Note also that the graph conveys the Mass which respondents say they most frequently attend, which is of course constrained by what is actually available. Accordingly, if based on actual liturgical preference/pastoral efficacy, we would expect this long tail to include an even bigger share of regular Mass-goers. Naturally, most of Britain's Eastern Catholics don't have the luxury of a weekly Sunday service in their own tradition. The same applies for others too.

Figure 1: Most frequently attended 'type' of Mass among weekly church-attending Catholics in Britain

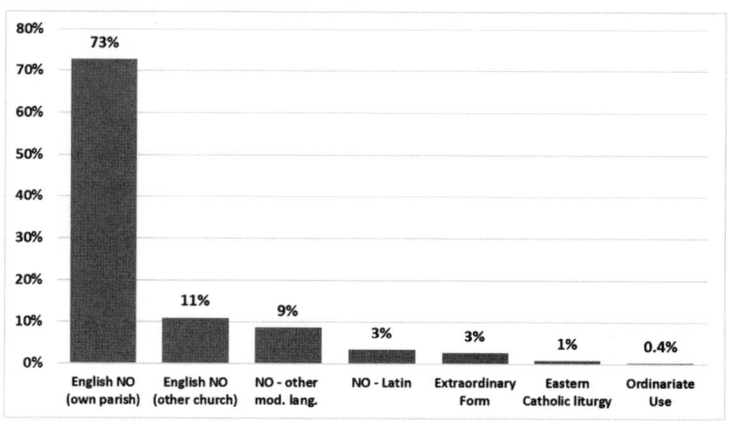

Source: Catholics in Britain 2019 (weighted data)

'Balkanisation' or *'Biodiversity'*?

Here we come to the crux of the matter. There is one school of thought which sees the 'liturgical long tail' as a kind of nefarious, ecclesial balkanisation, dividing up the Body of Christ into self-referential communities, who thus wall themselves off from the Church's true catholicity (as paradigmatically expressed by an 'ordinary parish Mass' at which all Catholics within given geographical boundaries gather 'as one'). Exceptions may, of course, be made for Eastern Catholics, who have legitimate reasons for congregating at a dedicated Mass/Divine Liturgy/*Qurbana* – at least in theory. (*In practice*, such communities, even when locally numerous, often struggle to be granted borrowed space in a diocesan church, hence their very reasonable desire for a 'church of one's own'.) Some allowances might also be made for particular linguistic groups, especially where these would otherwise be impeded from attaining 'that fully conscious, and active participation in liturgical celebrations which is demanded by the very nature of the liturgy'.[44] Even here, however, such groups are often encouraged – implicitly or otherwise – to 'integrate' as much, and as soon, as is possible. Their having 'their own' liturgies is seen as a hopefully temporary concession to pastoral necessity, rather than as something that should be encouraged to take root and thrive as a good thing in and of itself. Meanwhile, those groups who (wish to) gather around a valid and licit liturgical niche that *isn't* granted one of these 'ethnic exceptions' – the Ordinariate's Divine Worship, or the Extraordinary Form being the most obvious examples here – are most likely to bear the brunt of a misplaced desire to equate ecclesial unity with liturgical uniformity. Those who, for whatever reasons, find themselves best able to 'take part fully aware of what they are doing, actively

---

[44] *Sacrosanctum Concilium*, §14.

engaged in the rite, and enriched by its effects'[45] in these kinds of Masses are thus often dismissed as 'elitist', 'cliquey', 'divisive', or 'sectarian'. Perhaps, in some such congregations, there is indeed some truth to these characterisations, though they are assuredly not the norm. Moreover, we dare say that cliquiness, elitism, and the like can occur in more mainstream areas of the Church's pastoral life too.

Instead of 'balkanisation', we suggest that it is far better to think of liturgical long tails as evincing something rather more like (to leave behind economic metaphors for the moment) *biodiversity*, and to recognise how the genuine mutual flourishing of different groups – whether as personal parishes, shrine churches, or as regular and established congregations using space in parishes – benefits not just each group, but the entire ecclesial ecosystem. A diverse ecosystem is usually a healthy one for all involved. Liturgical niches are thus to be actively encouraged and organised for, rather than (at best) tolerated and accommodated. Our main reasons for thinking this are fivefold.

1. The first and most obvious follows from the simple fact that, as *Sacrosanctum Concilium* well recognises, different people are best helped along in their spiritual lives by different licit liturgical options. (Incidentally, this includes the possibility of actively participating in more than one 'type' of liturgy on a regular or semi-regular basis). Furthermore, given the painful fact that millions of baptised Catholics aren't regularly 'enriched' by the 'effects' of *any* Mass at all, then we perhaps ought to be glad of *any* legitimate liturgy that clearly helps at least some people to be so, or to be so more regularly.

---

[45] *Sacrosanctum Concilium*, § 11, <https://www.vatican.va/archive/hist_councils/ii_vatican_council/documents/vat-ii_const_19631204_sacrosanctum-concilium_en.html>.

2. As noted in chapter four, humans are social beings, and a good deal of our religious and spiritual lives is socially influenced and supported. There is much sociological and psychological evidence for thinking that densely networked congregations – i.e., 'Where everyone knows your name, and they're always glad you came' – are better at inculcating religious commitment in their members than are ones where people tend not to know many people.[46] There's another large body of scholarship suggesting that, on average, people naturally tend to gravitate towards people they have something in common with – e.g., with shared interests, shared life situations (parents of young families, say), shared cultural backgrounds.[47] Taking these factors together, it's easy to see why the liturgical long tail might be specially good at fostering the kinds of true *communities* that people often lament are absent (or at least less present than they might be, and once were) from ordinary parish life.

3. Relatedly, the kinds of people who are willing regularly to drive upwards of an hour on a Sunday to attend a specific liturgy in the middle of nowhere, rather than going to the parish five minutes down the road, *ipso facto* have to be highly committed to their Faith. And of course, once they find themselves in the same room together, then they (along with their respective children, *and* the more locally-based people who happen to drop in one Sunday because, say, noon is a convenient time, or because they've heard good things) all start to influence and encourage each other in being so committed. This type of in-group intensification has been well-studied in various spheres, from political partisanship to pop

---

[46] E.g., Matthew Facciani and Matthew E. Brashears, 'Sacred Alters: The Effects of Ego Network Structure on Religious and Political Beliefs', *Socius* 5 (2019), 1–16; James C. Cavendish, Michael R. Welch, and David C. Leege, 'Social Network Theory and Predictors of Religiosity for Black and White Catholics: Evidence of a "Black Sacred Cosmos"?', *Journal for the Scientific Study of Religion* 37/3 (1999), 397–410.

[47] See Miller McPherson, Lynn Smith-Lovin, and James M. Cook, "Birds of a Feather: Homophily in Social Networks," *Annual Review of Sociology* 27 (2001), 415–44.

culture fandoms,[48] and is a frequent by-product of long tails. This basic observation is one we have repeated several times throughout this book. Niche liturgical gatherings can thus help to incubate a seriously intentional faith in a way that is sometimes more difficult in other settings.

4. The commitment that one typically finds within the liturgical long tail *doesn't* stay within its 'silo': it spills over into the wider Church, including into 'ordinary' parish life. Many of those going to a niche Mass do not do so every single week. In fact, we suspect that, in practice, there are very few attendees who only, or almost only, worship within 'their' specific group. Even those fortunate to have a stable worshipping community sufficiently close will likely also be embedded within the life and worship of their 'home' diocesan parishes in various ways as well. Such people will often also be active in various wider groups within Catholic life – schools, youth movements, pro-life and social justice initiatives, fraternal organisations, university chaplaincies. We would also be willing to make a modest bet that the liturgical long tail significantly punches above its numerical weight in contributing practising Catholic adults, and moreover vocations, to the next generation. Some of these, of course, may well 'stay within' their niches – not a bad thing in itself, of course – but we suspect that most, even while keeping one foot in, do not. Thus caring for the long tail looks to be a good strategy for those playing the pastoral long game.

5. Finally, in those areas with an oversupply of churches (and thus with clergy and worshippers spread thinly over them), the liturgical long tail can perhaps offer a neat solution to pastoral planning-induced headaches. Rather than dioceses closing historic,

---

[48] See, e.g., Cass R. Sunstein, *Going to Extremes: How Like Minds Unite and Divide* (New York: Oxford University Press, 2009); Cass R. Sunstein, *Conformity: The Power of Social Influences* (New York: New York University Press, 2019); and Patrick Edwards, Daniel P. Chadborn, Courtney N. Plante, Stephen Reysen, and Marsh Howze Redden, *Meet the Bronies: The Psychology of the Adult My Little Pony Fandom* (Jefferson, NC: McFarland, 2019).

downtown churches and having them turned into luxury condos or hipster bars, niche groups could be loaned or given them to renovate and 'make a go of'. Sometimes they will fail after a few years, failing to attract sufficient worshippers (and donors) to be able to stand on their own two feet. So be it – *then*, if necessary, let the developers pave paradise and put in a parking lot. But often, we dare say, the results will be more *Field of Dreams* than *Big Yellow Taxi*: if you (re)build it, they will come. We have highlighted several such success stories in these pages; we know of plenty more. As is common in the liturgical long tail, these churches appear to draw their congregations from over a wide geographical area (with the vast majority of them remaining part, and often a valuable part, of their home parishes too), so the 'net loss' to any one ordinary parish's attendance is small. Meanwhile, the parishioners who used to attend Mass at those churches before either still do, or else have no shortage of nearby – walkably so, in some cases – 'normal' parishes of which to boost the numbers.

Conclusion

This is a chapter of two unequal halves. The first, and longer, surveyed the main contours of Britain's Latin Mass scene. This is a far more visible (some might add vocal) group than many of those we have looked at in this book. But, like them, it is not one that has received much research attention. Also like them, it is a site of relative resilience, strength, and hope. The future of British Catholicism will not *be* liturgical traditionalism, but liturgical traditionalism is certainly a part of that future. Even at present, it probably makes a disproportionately large contribution to vocations, both directly to traditionalist orders (the FSSP alone has ordained fifteen men from the UK in the past twenty-two years, and currently has more British men in formation than many dioceses), and – this is something often missed – in playing an important role in the liturgical, theological, and spiritual formation of many of those joining seminaries or congregations such as the Benedictines, Dominicans, and Oratorians. The numbers of children at Latin Masses, sometimes outnumbering the adults, and the comparatively high levels of family religious practice, also more or less guarantee that they will punch above their (modest) weight as contributors to the next generation of practising Catholics.

The second, shorter half has advanced a much larger, and more theoretical argument, bringing together a number of themes explored at various points in this and the previous chapters. The basic argument here is that a diverse ecosystem of distinctive ecclesial 'niches', such as we in fact see in British Catholicism (especially when one is looking for particular trend-bucking areas of strength), is a good thing, not only for the specific groups themselves, but for the greater good too.

One potential downside of how we have structured this book with five thematic case-studies – parishes, young adult initiatives, diasporic communities, universities, Trads – is that it might give the impression that any of these is somehow cut off, either from each other, of from the Church as a whole. Nothing could be further from the truth. For one thing, British Catholicism is not a big enough world for any one subworld to exist 'entire of itself'. Indeed, at many times during our fieldwork we have found our case-studies overlapping. Let us give just one example here. In summer 2019, the charismatic young adult group Youth 2000's festival in Walsingham happened to fall on the same weekend as the Latin Mass Society's annual walking pilgrimage from London. Viewed through a certain, surface-level lens, these are polar opposites: liturgically, culturally. Viewed less superficially, they are very close to each other indeed. Both put a premium on Confession, Adoration, the Holy Mass; devotion to the Saints, and pro-life zeal was in evidence at both. Both involved, and indeed made a virtue out of, enduring physical and material discomfort for both spiritual and social ends (camping in a field with portaloos for Y2K-ers, walking tens of miles for successive days for the LMS pilgrims). More to the point, there were several people from the Youth 2000 event who nevertheless opted for Sunday Mass in the Extraordinary Form across the road. Many more, from either group, would have looked perfectly in place at the other one. The early-20s girl in jeans, a Harry Potter t-shirt, and a mantilla at the LMS Mass would have been among friends in the Youth 2000 worship big-top. Literally so, in fact: one of her best friends from university was one of the volunteers.

6. Epilogue: A British Spring?

We started this book with a rainy day in spring 2019, which also happened to be the first piece of fieldwork we did for it. We finish writing it on another rainy day, also in spring, in 2024. There is a pleasing symmetry to this, at least for those who know their history of hoped-for revivals in the Church's fortunes.

Preaching to the recently 'restored' Catholic bishops of England and Wales in 1852, St John Henry Newman offered a stirring vision of better days ahead. He begins by noting the cyclical pattern of the natural world:

> [T]hough it is ever dying, it is ever coming to life again… Dissolution does but give birth to fresh modes of organisation, and one death is the parent of a thousand lives… The sun sinks to rise again; the day is swallowed up in the gloom of night, to be born out of it, as fresh as if it had never been quenched. Spring passes into summer, and through summer and autumn into winter, only the more surely, by its own ultimate return, to triumph over that grave, towards which it resolutely hastened from its first hour.[1]

Such is not, however, the normal run of things in the sphere of human history: 'Powers of the world, sovereignties, dynasties, sooner or later come to nought; they have their fatal hour…

---

[1] John Henry Newman, 'The Second Spring', in *Sermons Preached on Various Occasions* (London: Burns and Lambert, 1858), 221–70.

Thus man and all his works are mortal; they die, and they have no power of renovation.'[2]

And so, he continues, had it seemed for the Catholic Church, which had once 'stood in this land in pride of place... the honours of near a thousand years upon it',[3] but had been laid to near-ruin in the three centuries following the Reformation. His description of 'the utter contempt into which Catholicism had fallen' is worth quoting at length (not least for those despairing overmuch at our current predicament):

> No longer the Catholic Church in the country; nay, no longer, I may say, a Catholic community;—but a few adherents of the Old Religion, moving silently and sorrowfully about, as memorials of what had been. "The Roman Catholics";—not a sect, not even an interest, as men conceived of it,—not a body, however small, representative of the great communion abroad,—but a mere handful of individuals, who might be counted, like the pebbles and *detritus* of the great deluge, and who, forsooth, merely happened to retain a creed which, in its day indeed, was the profession of a Church. Here a set of poor Irishmen, coming and going at harvest time, or a colony of them lodged in a miserable quarter of the vast metropolis. There, perhaps an elderly person, seen walking in the streets, grave and solitary, and strange, though noble in bearing, and said to be of good family, and—a "Roman Catholic". An old fashioned house of gloomy appearance, closed in with high walls, with an iron gate, and yews, and the report attaching to it that "Roman Catholics" lived there; but who they were, or what they did, or what was meant by calling them Roman Catholics, no one could tell;—though it had an unpleasant sound, and told of form and superstition...

[2] Ibid., 226.
[3] Ibid.

EPILOGUE: A BRITISH SPRING?

> Such were Catholics in England, found in corners, and alleys, and cellars, and the housetops, or in the recesses of the country; cut off from the populous world around them, and dimly seen, as if through a mist or in twilight, as ghosts flitting to and fro, by the high Protestants, the lords of the earth.[4]

In the usual run of human history, there would be no reason to suppose that such a community should suddenly revive. Religions, unlike the sun, do not fall and rise again on a set schedule. Churches don't operate according to the seasons, and England had its springtime in the centuries following St Augustine of Canterbury's mission. There is no reason, *a priori*, to expect another.

And yet, that is precisely what, in Newman's day, appeared to be occurring. Hence the famous title of his sermon: 'The Second Spring'.

> But what is it, my Fathers, my Brothers, what is it that has happened in England just at this time? Something strange is passing over this land, by the very surprise, by the very commotion, which it excites...
>
> The past *has* returned, the dead lives. Thrones are overturned, and are never restored; States live and die, and then are matter only for history. Babylon was great, and Tyre, and Egypt, and Nineve, and shall never be great again. The English Church was, and the English Church was not, and the English Church is once again. This is the portent, worthy of a cry. It is the coming in of a Second Spring; it is a restoration in the moral world, such as that which yearly takes place in the physical.[5]

★★★

---

[4] Ibid., 232–4.
[5] Ibid., 226, 229.

A book such as ours, advancing a hopeful 'it is always darkest just before the day dawneth'[6] case for Catholicism in Britain (not alone England), could scarcely resist citing Newman's 'second spring' at some point. In truth, we feel that we've been rather restrained. We might have titled the book *Third Spring!*, and opened it not with a rainy day in West Bromwich, but with a sunny day in Vatican City: Newman's canonisation in October 2019, another of our early fieldtrips. But that, we fear, would have been rather too optimistic – indeed, much too fate-tempting.

We have made two main predictions in these pages: a) Catholic decline will definitely *not* continue 'down to zero', but before too long will bottom out; and then b) from a fairly solid base, it will start to grow again, if gradually. While these predictions are, we believe, well-founded ones, neither should make anyone feel complacent. For one thing, precisely 'when' and 'how high/low' the bottom will be is in no sense fore-ordained, and these two 'To Be Confirmeds' will have a critical influence over how sustainable the resulting upturn will be. Obviously, the *sooner* and *higher* they are, the better the longer term will be. And this is precisely why we have focussed in so much detail on so many and varied signs of hope within the Church. These groups, and others like them, will have an outsized role to play: directly, in helping to produce and sustain committed British Catholics; and indirectly, in offering other areas of the Church encouragement and examples of 'best practice' that might profitably be borrowed and adapted.

Better days may be coming, but they won't necessarily be easy ones. 'Late secularisation'[7] is not an easy situation for any religious community, even though we suspect that over time it will generate considerable evangelistic opportunities of its own. Cultural

---

[6] Thomas Fuller, *A Pisgah Sight of Palestine and the Confines Thereof; With the History of the Old and New Testaments Acted Thereon* (London: William Tegg, [1650] 1869), 208.

[7] Steve Bruce, 'Late Secularization and Religion as Alien', *Open Theology* 1 (2014), 13–23.

EPILOGUE: A BRITISH SPRING?

Christianity is not without its merits, but it does mean that a lot of people raised in it receive exposure to many weak or dead strains of Christianity, effectively inoculating them against ever catching a live one. This breeds societies with significant 'herd immunity' to the gospel. Past a certain point of secularising, however, then feasibly this will no longer be the case. At such a time people may it find easier to encounter the good news as something genuinely new. Even so, much of this progress will be uphill.

Given this, the following passage from Newman's 'Second Spring' is one that might be worth remembering (replacing 'British' for 'English' throughout).

> But still, could we be surprised... if the winter even now should not yet be quite over? Have we any right to take it strange, if, in this English land, the spring-time of the Church should turn out to be an English spring; an uncertain, anxious time of hope and fear, of joy and suffering,—of bright promise and budding hopes, yet withal of keen blasts, and cold showers, and sudden storms?[8]

All this lies in the future, though. If this little book has any single take-home message, it is that British Catholicism has a future.

---

[8] Newman, 'Second Spring', 244.

Appendix: Historical Mass attendance statistics

Year	England & Wales	Scotland	Britain (i.e., combined)
1950		420,250	
1951			
1952			
1953			
1954			
1955			
1956			
1957			
1958	1,874,233		
1959	1,892,100		
1960	1,949,400	382,110	2,331,510
1961	2,024,000		
1962	2,092,667		
1963			
1964			
1965	2,114,219		
1966	2,091,856		
1967	2,055,254		
1968	1,987,880		
1969	1,934,853		
1970	1,899,803	311,000	2,210,803
1971	1,885,960		
1972	1,831,550		

APPENDIX: HISTORICAL MASS ATTENDANCE STATISTICS

Year	England & Wales	Scotland	Britain (i.e., combined)
1973			
1974	1,752,759		
1975	1,790,980		
1976	1,722,210		
1977	1,698,836		
1978	1,694,175		
1979	1,674,562		
1980	1,644,224	296,030	1,940,254
1981			
1982	1,570,230		
1983	1,536,902		
1984	1,512,553		
1985	1,459,947		
1986	1,424,507		
1987	1,398,782		
1988	1,383,627		
1989	1,350,459		
1990	1,323,301	283,546	1,606,847
1991	1,299,685	272,642	1,572,327
1992		268,508	
1993	1,277,617	253,528	1,531,145
1994	1,226,197	250,142	1,476,339
1995	1,190,307	248,935	1,439,242
1996	1,135,047	239,232	1,374,279
1997	1,086,268	235,613	1,321,881
1998	1,056,027	227,654	1,283,681
1999	1,041,728	222,956	1,264,684
2000	1,005,522	212,241	1,217,763
2001	994,181	213,284	1,207,465
2002	1,071,975	204,645	1,276,620

Year	England & Wales	Scotland	Britain (i.e., combined)
2003		194,728	
2004	958,541	193,939	1,152,480
2005	941,208	192,235	1,133,443
2006	927,154	192,463	1,119,617
2007	915,556	184,283	1,099,839
2008	918,844	185,608	1,104,452
2009	898,852	175,029	1,073,881
2010	885,169	170,894	1,056,063
2011		160,867	
2012	848,960	161,961	1,010,921
2013		157,649	
2014		149,106	
2015		144,330	
2016	772,123	135,705	907,828
2017	739,317	135,518	874,835
2018	712,909	130,128	843,037
2019	701,902	127,003	828,905
2020*		38,356	
2021*	389,960	72,724	462,684
2022	503,008	89,420	592,428

* Covid-19 pandemic years.

NB: This is an updated, corrected, and expanded version of the figures published in Stephen Bullivant, *Mass Exodus: Catholic Disaffiliation in Britain and America since Vatican II* (Oxford: Oxford University Press, 2019), 265-9. Figures have been collated over a period of years from a wide range of official and academic sources. These include:

Bishops' Conference of Scotland. 1996-2024. *The Catholic Directory for Scotland* (Glasgow: Burns' Publications)

APPENDIX: HISTORICAL MASS ATTENDANCE STATISTICS

Brierley, Peter (ed.). 1999. *Religious Trends 2000/1* (London: Marshall Pickering)

Bruce, Steve. 2014. *Scottish Gods: Religion in Modern Scotland 1900–2012* (Edinburgh: Edinburgh University Press)

Kinnear, Tim. 2024. 'Statistical Appendices', in Alana Harris (ed.), *The Oxford History of British and Irish Catholicism, Vol. 5: Recapturing the Apostolate of the Laity, 1914–2021* (Oxford: Oxford University Press), 357-76

Latin Mass Society. 2013. 'Newly released statistics show the decline of the Catholic Church in England and Wales in 1960s and 1970s', available online: https://lms.org.uk/statistics (last accessed 12 September 2023)

Spencer, Anthony E. C. W. 2014. 'An Assessment of the Catholic Statistics in the 2014 Edition of the Catholic Directory. Part II. Mass Attendance, Baptisms, Marriages & Receptions', available online: <https://www.prct.org.uk/blogs>

For recent data, we are especially indebted to Lorraine Welch at the Catholic Bishops' Conference for England and Wales, and Fr Alfie McKenzie, editor of *The Catholic Directory for Scotland*.